Aren't You Glad You Read This?

AREN'T YOU YOU GLAD YOU READ THIS?

THE COMPLETE HOW-TO GUIDE FOR SINGLES WITH A
HISTORY OF FAILED RELATIONSHIPS WHO WANT
THEIR NEXT RELATIONSHIP TO SUCCEED

ERICA GORDON

THOUGHT
CATALOG
Books

BROOKLYN, NY

THOUGHT CATALOG Books

Published by Thought Catalog Books, a division of The Thought & Expression Co., Williamsburg, Brooklyn. Founded in 2010, Thought Catalog is a website and imprint dedicated to your ideas and stories. We publish fiction and non-fiction from emerging and established writers across all genres. For general information and submissions: manuscripts@thoughtcatalog.com.

First edition, 2017

ISBN: 978-1945796395

Printed and bound in the United States.

10 9 8 7 6 5 4 3 2 1

CONTENTS

Introduction

This book is for all the single men and women who have experienced a series of failed relationships, have *not* had great luck when it comes to dating and need some eye-opening, brutally honest advice before they'll be truly ready to get back out there.

Perhaps you've been single for quite some time, you've been avoiding the dating world because you were exhausted by it in the past, and you're finally considering trying again.

Maybe you were sabotaging your previous relationships in order to keep them casual, but now you're ready for something real.

Then there are those who aren't sure why they've had such bad luck in love, haven't necessarily been single by choice, and all they know is that they want their next shot at it to work. Whether you were single by choice or single by misfortune, the fact remains that you're now ready for something meaningful.

It's normal to be confused about why all of your relationships go nowhere or to wonder what you've been doing wrong.

If your friends are getting engaged or getting serious with someone while you remain strangely unfulfilled or lonely, you might be thinking about giving dating another shot. Yes, *dating*, not hooking up.

Aren't You Glad You Read This? is an attitude-transforming, perspective-altering, smart, and honest how-to guide for singles who have a history of relationship failures and want their next relationship to succeed. It's about time you figured out where you've been going wrong, got out of your funk, and found the confidence and the happiness you're worthy of.

You deserve to find something real, and it's completely normal if you've been dating for five, ten, even twenty years and haven't found it yet. If you're 30 and single this book is for you. If you're 50 and single, this book is for you. It doesn't matter how long you've had bad luck for, because all that means is that you've had time to work on you, and now something great is coming your way.

Maybe you're reading this because dating hasn't been working out for you and you've dealt with an overwhelming amount of rejection or missed opportunities. Stay single for now and just read this because there are some things you need to know before you begin a new relationship.

In this book, you'll get valuable guidance on relationships at the *right* time, which is—you guessed it—*before* you start one. Relationship advice is the most beneficial before you enter a new relationship because this way you're reading it before it's too late. You're currently a clean slate, ready to be prepped for what could be the best love story of your life.

The True Meaning Of 'Timing Is Everything'

There's nothing worse than knowing
that you're probably perfect for each other,
just not right now.
—*Anonymous*

In this book, we'll unavoidably touch on a few of those annoying dating clichés that you hear time and time again, dive into what they really mean and discuss whether or not there's any truth to them.

Timing is everything is a dating cliché that holds a lot of truth. It's incredibly perplexing when someone is a total catch, yet can't seem to keep anyone interested and has experienced failed relationship after failed relationship. If you're a great catch, why does your dating history insinuate that you've never quite been good enough? If you're the whole package—why haven't you found true love?

This dating paradox is more common than you think. Most

of the time, it happens because you're holding yourself back. Whether you're aware of it or unaware of it, you've been sabotaging any chance at love that comes your way.

Your dating failures weren't due to you not being good enough; you were just always standing in your own way, that's all. Your perceived inadequacy was probably the only vice that made you ill-equipped to be in a successful relationship.

Perhaps you were self-sabotaging due to imbedded insecurities, a psychological attachment to failure, low self-worth or a lack of self-confidence.

There's a very big difference between wanting a relationship and being ready for one. Those who want a relationship because they think it will make them feel whole aren't fit for one yet. The timing isn't right for these people, because they still have a lot of self-discovery to do and they would simply be using the relationship as an escape from that self-reflection or as a way of masking their inner pain. Your partner might be one giant Band-Aid, but your wounds are still underneath even if they're temporarily buried.

That's why it's much more important to love yourself than to be loved by someone else. Bettering your relationship with yourself is what will change your life, not finding the perfect partner.

The fact that someone else loves you
doesn't rescue you from the project
of loving yourself.
—Sahaj Kohli

Those with insecurities have warped ideas on what being in a relationship should be like. They look to their partner to provide them with confidence, reassurance, positivity, validation, happiness and direction. They rely on their partner too much, which is one of the main reasons why some relationships never stand a chance.

The concept of *timing is everything* comes into play when you enter a stage of your life where you truly begin to love yourself. Perhaps it's because you've found your calling, discovered your gift, developed healthier lifestyle habits, gotten to know yourself better, gained self-confidence and realized your worth.

It is at this point that your next relationship is (finally) likely to be a successful one.

Through identifying with the things in life that bring you joy, and by truly being happy single, you've proven that you're ready for a partnership because you have now taken the pressure off of your partner to make you happy. By not being reliant on him or her for your happiness, you're ensuring that they won't feel suffocated, overwhelmed or stuck.

When you reach this healthy state of mind, you'll stop projecting your insecurities and you'll start exuding confidence, which is one of the top qualities both men and women seek in their counterpart.

Most people prefer to be with someone who has other things in life that make them happy, other significant chapters in their story and much more going for them than just this relationship.

Below, you'll find a checklist. If you find yourself checking almost all of the boxes, it's safe to say that the 'time' to begin a new relationship is now—and you're truly ready for something meaningful.

How to Be Sure that You're Truly Ready for a Relationship

> *The whole point of being alive*
> *is to evolve into the complete person*
> *you were intended to be.*
> —Oprah Winfrey

The time to enter into a new relationship is now, as long as you're checking most of these boxes:

☐ You agree that the reward of being in love is worth the risk of heartbreak and the sacrifices of time and effort.

☐ Your behaviour while single isn't drastically different from how it would be if you were in a relationship.

☐ You have several hobbies and interests that make you happy—especially when you enjoy them alone.

☐ You want a relationship, but you don't feel you *need* one to be happy; you're already a happy and optimistic person.

☐ You've discovered your gift.

☐ You're not overly guarded, nor do you have walls up.

☐ You are unfulfilled by casual sex.

☐ You're sick of the hookup culture and seeking intimacy instead.

☐ You're confident and comfortable in your own skin.

☐ You're established in a career that you love.

☐ You've found your calling and your passion in life.

☐ You've found a purpose.

☐ You're accepting of yourself and have high self-worth,

☐ Independent,

☐ Financially stable, and

☐ Mentally well or aware of shortcomings.

☐ You're over your ex and you're not 'hung up' on anyone.

☐ You're bored of surface-level and casual relationships.

☐ You're in a healthy relationship with yourself.

☐ You aren't feeling empty, but you're feeling as though something might be missing.

☐ You're not shallow—you can look past looks and find value in personality and other non-physical qualities.

☐ You're reliant on yourself, not on others,

☐ Open to dating outside of your 'type,' and

☐ Already accomplished and already have devoted plenty of time to yourself.

☐ You intend to be faithful and monogamous.

☐ You resolve conflicts maturely.

☐ You're willing to take a risk and give up other options.

☐ You view an amazing relationship as a reward for sacrificing those options.

☐ You're empathetic to the feelings of others.

☐ You have reasonable expectations of a significant other.

☐ You're not a push-over—you stand up for what you believe in.

☐ You're a grateful and positive person rather than a negative person.

☐ Rejection no longer breaks you—you've developed thick skin and resilience

☐ You communicate directly and openly.

☐ You've been single long enough, and you've gotten the single life out of your system.

☐ You are capable of having a good time while sober.

☐ You're well-rounded with hobbies, friends, career, etc.

☐ You've reflected on your mistakes and thought about what's gone wrong.

☐ You truly believe that you are a catch.

☐ You know what you want.

☐ You're ambitious and goal-oriented.

☐ You're emotionally available.

☐ Commitment doesn't scare you.

☐ You think stability is comforting, not boring.

☐ You know what being in a romantic relationship means and what it comes with.

☐ You have high standards for how you deserve to be treated.

Did you notice how many of the qualities on the above checklist involve things like having found your passion in life and having discovered your gift? That's because your journey in life isn't just about finding love. It's about recognizing that there might be milestones in your life that are just as significant as (perhaps even more significant than) finding love. Finding a lasting partnership is only one chapter of your life's story, which is why you need to refrain from putting too much pressure on the pursuit of love. Remind yourself that finding someone isn't the be-all-end-all of your life because once you take the pressure off of the pursuit of a relationship, you'll have a much easier time both finding one and being in one.

2

Your Relationship With Yourself Sets The Bar For Every Relationship In Your Life

*If you're still looking for that one person
who can change your life,
take a look in the mirror.*
—Roman Price

I'm sure you've wondered what type of partner your perfect match is seeking. There are certain qualities in particular that transcend all others such as self-love and being able to self-validate. Let me explain:

Here's What Happens to your Romantic Relationships When You Don't Love Yourself

When your state of mind is clouded with insecurities and feelings of inadequacy, your romantic relationships will be doomed and dysfunctional. When you don't love yourself, you might find that spending time with your partner can make your pain go away. Your pain returns, however, when they're not around to distract you. Since your inner pain hasn't been properly dealt with it will manifest as desperation which will seep into and destroy your relationship.

Your insecurities are more influential on your partner than you think. You'll exhaust your partner with your constant need for validating attention and reassurance, and your low self-esteem will wear on your partner as he or she continuously witnesses your inner struggles.

Self-love is learned and practiced. Without first mastering self-love, your romantic relationships will suffer a noticeable disconnect. When you both love yourselves, however, you'll be able to establish a genuine connection.

By not loving yourself, you're creating extra work for your partner.

When you struggle with self-doubt and low self-esteem, your partner will have to work extra hard to make you happy. In order to make you smile, feel good, or feel loved, they'll have to exhaust themselves. Sometimes, despite their best efforts to give you validation, positivity, love, and support—it won't be enough for you. Imagine how frustrating that would be and understand that eventually, they'll probably leave you because of it.

When you don't love yourself, you imagine that things are worse than they actually are.

People who don't love themselves tend to imagine that things are going terribly in the relationship—that things are worse than they are. That's simply them projecting their insecurities. Rejection reinforces insecurities, so the more times you're rejected the more times you'll get rejected—again and again. Why? Because insecurities aren't attractive.

By believing in negative outcomes, you're attracting negative outcomes.

When you don't love yourself, you accept poor treatment.

Do you have friends who let their partner walk all over them? Doesn't it frustrate you when you're forced to witness their acceptance of poor treatment? That's what happens when someone enters into a relationship before they've fallen in love with themselves. They'll accept abusive, neglectful, or poor treatment because they don't believe that they're deserving of better. The most intuitive people are the ones who avoid dating and relationships until they love themselves because they intuitively know that this is the only way they'll attract a partner who treats them right.

The longer it takes you to love yourself, the less "sticky" you'll be.

I love this sticker analogy I came up with. It's pretty original (so don't use it without quoting me, please.) Imagine a brand new sticker that hasn't been used yet. (Maybe this was you as a child.) It's untouched, undamaged, unattached, and in perfect condition. It's super sticky. You could stick it onto anything, and you would form a strong bond and happily stay put.

However, every time you (the once-untouched sticker) gets rejected, undervalued, caught up in self-hate, or accepts a relationship where someone isn't treating you right, you lose some of your stickiness.

We (the stickers) get less sticky every time we engage in negative thoughts, self-hate, self-sabotage, or dysfunctional relationships. *Especially* from engaging in dysfunctional relationships.

The problem with losing your stickiness is that each time you attempt to stick onto someone new, it gets easier and easier to pull away because connections become harder and harder to form. When you've lost your stickiness due prolonged self-doubt and incessant insecurities, you might still feel a connection with someone, but it probably won't stick.

Just like a sticker that's been used and abused, we don't form as strong connections as we once did. But if there was ever a way to somehow get sticky again, it would be through self-improving and self-betterment. The only way to escape this pattern of failure and heartbreak is to work on your relationship with yourself. When it comes to your history of bad luck in love, the solution is internal and not external. The antidote comes from within.

It's only when you truly love yourself that you can bring positivity into a relationship.

It's usually those who have issues with themselves who bring negativity into their relationships. Negativity is extremely unattractive, and anyone who brings negative thoughts into their relationships is guaranteed to lose their partner's interest quite quickly.

Whether you realize it or not, your dysfunctional relationship with yourself is almost always going to be the reason your relationships don't work out.

Why *Not* Needing Validation from your Partner is One of the Most Attractive Qualities You Can Possess

A huge perk that comes with self-love is the ability to self-validate. There's something sexy and intriguing about a person who doesn't require validation from their partner. Imagine dating someone strong and independent who doesn't need constant reassurance, nor do they feel the need to have the relationship broadcast all over social media. They trust in what you have with each other, they're not concerned with what others think, and they're secure with both themselves and with where the relationship is heading.

When you don't require validation, you draw others in with your confidence because you always seem so sure of yourself.

Self-confidence and security don't stem from the approval of others, they come from within. They build from having passions, interests, plans and stories—and from knowing who you are. It's your inherent ability to feel confident without the help of external, confidence-boosting triggers. That's what makes your particular tenacity so unique and special. You're always optimistic even when things aren't quite going your way, and somehow you get others to see things your way simply due to how certain you come across.

Those who validate themselves have a better understanding of who they are and therefore, they have a stronger identity and less erratic emotions.

They're independent and able to be their true selves without reservations. Through this, they're able to give more of themselves to their partner than someone who was struggling with identity issues could.

What helped me immensely with my identity issues was discovering my gift. For me, it was discovering that I can write. I love writing and I'm good at it, which is why I so easily identify with the role and make a healthy living doing it. Discovering my gift (and love for) writing helped me start to love myself, and it helped me self-validate instead of seeking validation from others. It was actually Steve Harvey who made me realize how powerful having (and using) a gift can be. In Steve Harvey's book *Act Like A Success, Think Like A Success* he points out:

> *You will miss out on the true blessing of your life if you don't accept that your gift is your winning ticket and the key to your life's blessings. All you have to do is commit to your gift. Once you commit, the rest of it—the money, the connections, and the opportunities—will start coming to you in ways that your can't imagine.*

Steve Harvey may be a big reason why I decided to commit to writing full time. I committed to my gift full time, and my self-love grew tremendously. I found that the opportunities that came my way through writing distracted me from wanting a relationship and distracted me from noticing that I had been single for over five years. Seriously, I barely noticed. That's saying something considering I was about to be 30 and single which is supposed to be a horrifying thought. When I did start dating, my gift was still my main focus, and that helped me to not get caught up in the typical fears and anxieties someone would often have when they're keeping tabs on their partner or focusing more on their partner than on themselves.

Self-validation also helps you care a little bit less. That's not to say that you shouldn't care about your partner—of course you should. But caring less about each and every little thing he or she does wrong will help your relationship in the long run.

Sometimes, the reason why someone doesn't require validation from his or her partner is because they're getting plenty of validation elsewhere. They're respected in their workplace, they're admired by their peers, and they wake up each morning feeling confident in who they are and what they stand for. They've finally achieved self-actualization.

These secure and stable individuals tend to march to the beat of their own drum. They're both realists and dreamers, and they definitely don't pay much attention to the negative opinions of others.

This healthy state of mind keeps you from getting knocked down—and if you are knocked down, you'll land on your feet and hit the ground running again almost immediately. You're resilient and selective.

Selective? Yes. Those who don't require validation aren't

worried that they'll be judged for being perpetually single. They choose to wait until they find someone who they think is worth their time, and to hell with what anyone thinks about their prolonged singlehood.

The ability to get through life without needing validation allows you to truly be yourself, and one day, your partner is going to appreciate you *so much* for always being so real. You don't need to fit in, you don't need to stay in the box, you don't conform, and you don't feel the urge to please others all the time. Why? Because you don't care if people think you're doing or saying the right thing—you just want to do you. You have no problem saying no to people and you don't feel guilty standing up for yourself. That's exactly why you're so awesome.

Not requiring validation keeps you authentic because you're not always anxiously seeking approval. You're therefore never afraid to be yourself. This ensures that you'll meet someone who falls in love with the *real* you—not some fake, approval-seeking version of you.

Those who self-validate are rarely fake. They won't beat around the bush, sugarcoat things, or tell people what they want to hear so that they're liked. If you're like this, you'll probably never smile when you're feeling low just to avoid looking awkward. You'll always laugh when something is really funny. Everything about you is just *real*. Most people find that extremely attractive because they crave being around someone who is genuine—especially in this overly-filtered, often-phony world that we live in where truth is becoming extinct and is therefore highly sought after.

Would You Date Yourself? Why You Need to Become the Type of Person You Want to Meet

Ladies: you probably won't find Mr. Right until you become Mrs. Right first. And gentlemen, if you want to find Mrs. Right, you need to work on becoming Mr. Right first.

I chose to stay single for a long time because I knew that I had a lot of things to work on, and I knew that I wasn't Mrs. Right yet. I'm sure I was *someone's* Mrs. Right, but I have high standards and I definitely wasn't good enough yet for the type of man I wanted. The type of man I wanted was a man who might not think I was up to his standards. But I knew I could get to his standards, in time. So I stayed single, and I worked on me, and I worked on my blog The Babe Report, and I enjoyed being single.

That might sound strange, but the thing is that if you do have high standards (which you should) and you haven't yet become who you want to be (the best version of you) then you'll end up settling for someone below your standards. Why? Because you don't believe that you're good enough for the idealized partner you've been dreaming of.

We all have things we need to work on. For some of us, it's finding a career we love (and one we're good at.) For others, it's the self-love that isn't where it needs to be. And for still others, it's things like being at an unhealthy weight, having unhealthy habits, or having a substance abuse problem.

Being single gives you the time to face these problems and work on them. Once accomplished, you can think to yourself, "Anyone would be lucky to date me!" and that's when you're in a great position to start dating.

3

Finding 'The One'

> *There are far, far better things ahead*
> *than any we leave behind.*
> —C. S. Lewis

Finding 'the One' or letting 'the One' find you is dependent on you taking chances, letting your guard down, and risking everything. When you're guarded, no true connection can be formed, which is why the cliché *love like you've never been hurt* is heard so often. Even though you may have been hurt in the past, you can spin that hurt into hope by reminding yourself that there are better relationships ahead than any you left behind.

'The One' Can't Find You if You Stay Hidden

You have to stop hiding if you want to find love. Unfortunately, it's quite common for people to hide themselves away from the rest of the world if they're struggling emotionally. If you've

19

been hurt in the past, you have trouble with your self-confidence, you've dealt with a ton of rejection or you feel hopeless, you'll want to stay hidden because in hiding you feel safe.

It's in this state that you're trapping yourself behind metaphorical prison bars. These 'prison bars' can prevent you from reaching your full potential in life, and they keep you feeling inhibited when it comes to relationships.

It goes without saying that those who have a high self-worth, those who love themselves, and those who feel confident don't tend to hide out. Instead, they're comfortable with being seen, taking risks, and putting themselves out there.

Once you work on yourself and recognize your worth, you'll feel less trapped and more open to finding love. That self-limiting, insecure mindset that was keeping you locked up will be replaced with an open and confident mindset which positively changes your dating experiences.

If you've been in hiding because you're afraid of rejection, afraid of change, or weary of what's out there, change your attitude. Remember that even though you feel comfortable in hiding, the best things are going to be discovered once you stop worrying, get out there, and start living for today.

Bravery Will Get You Everywhere

Love is everything it's cracked up to be. It really is worth fighting for, being brave for, risking everything for.
—*Erica Jong*

In today's dating culture, bravery will put you miles ahead of your competition, especially since acts of bravery and bold moves are becoming rarer and rarer.

Being brave is old-fashioned, in a good way. Millennials are terrible at dating. We're the unromantic generation. Any old-fashioned lovers out there are doing it right. We could all learn a thing or two from them.

If you want to be in a relationship, bravery will get you there. If you're looking for a meaningful partnership, bravery will help you communicate those feelings before the opportunity is lost.

It's no secret that we're part of an unusually passive dating culture. The fear of rejection stops us from taking risks, but without taking risks, we'd all be single forever.

Rejection is nothing to fear. It's never personal, it's just an inevitable part of the process.

> *You can be the ripest, juiciest peach in the world,*
> *and there's still going to be someone who hates peaches.*
> *—Dita Von Teese*

By being brave in a world full of passive bystanders, you'll stand out. You'll get what you want. You won't let yourself or anyone else stand in your way.

The truth is what connects us.

Truth. Honesty. Authenticity. All these qualities are so much rarer than they should be. In relationships, instead of practicing truth, many of us are playing games. Instead of being honest about who we are and what we want, many of us are hiding behind a controlled image of ourselves that we've created to be perceived a certain way.

When you aren't afraid to show your weaknesses and you're fine with your partner catching you on a bad day, you're being genuine. When you're direct about your feelings instead of saying what you think they want to hear, you're showing that person that with you, they'll always know where they stand. There won't be any uncomfortable uncertainty with you.

You'll find that the more truth you share with someone, and the more real you are with them, the deeper your connection will be with that person and the more you'll stand out and outshine others in their path.

In fact, hiding behind a persona of who you think they want you to be will only get you farther and farther away from what you want: a meaningful and amazing relationship.

The truth is what lets you in, and it's the only way to avoid an otherwise inevitable disconnect.

A Permanent Vacation Mindset Will Help You Find 'The One'

Speaking of bravery, have you noticed how much braver you are when you're on vacation? The guarded types (the types who like to hide) all have one thing in common: all of that hiding and cautious deliberating goes out the window when they're on vacation. Why is that?

When you're in vacation mode, you'll become a different, better version of yourself—and that's why you tend to find romance in exotic places. It's not where you are, it's who you become when you're there.

The physical distance you've put between yourself and your hometown seems to work as a portal that lets you temporarily embody an idealized version of you. Suddenly, you have a pep in your step and you just *feel* happier and more alive. Perceptible distance can create a psychological distance, as well. You'll notice a separation from the lively vacation mode you and the more morose mentality you left at home.

None of this has to be temporary, though. The fun, carefree, and positive person you become when you're on vacation isn't someone who you have to leave in the tropics. You most certainly can and should bring that version of you home.

Single people tend to bank on a fun vacation hookup while they're away, knowing that it'll surely happen. Why is it that the vacationing version of you always has a much easier time meeting people than the regular you? When it comes to flirting, dating, romance, and hooking up, it all seems so effortless when you're away on holiday.

That laid back, in-the-moment, and opportunistic version of you shouldn't be reserved for vacations. No, the awesome vacation-mode you should come out to play a lot more often. If we adopted that I'm-on-vacation mentality every day, our love lives would stand to benefit a remarkable change. It's this holiday mindset that will get you everywhere when it comes to dating.

Here are some reasons why permanently adopting the vacation mindset will significantly change and improve your dating life:

1. You'll be bold and in-the-moment.

When you're on holiday, there's no past and there's no future. The only 'you' is the present you. You learn to live in the moment when you're away because you want to make the most of your short vacation.

This means that you appreciate everything a lot more, you take advantage of more opportunities, and you don't shy away from experiences.

If we adopted this mentality in our everyday lives, dating would be so much better.

2. You can be anyone you want to be.

When this playful, uninhibited, just-go-for-it version of you comes out on vacation, you begin to re-identify yourself in a very positive way. Instead of letting that new identity vanish when you get back home, try your best to keep the new you alive.

3. You'll throw inhibitions to the wind.

On vacation, you're less reserved, less inhibited, more outgoing, and more confident. You take advantage of every opportunity, you let loose, and you don't overthink everything that you do.

Feeling as though you have nothing to lose is a big plus of the holiday mindset, and if we kept that mentality going, we wouldn't lose out on similar opportunities back home. If back home we felt that we didn't have time to waste, we wouldn't let our insecurities get in the way of an opportunity to get out there and meet someone.

4. You'll seize each day.

It's the sense of time limitations that pushes us to seize each day when we're on vacation. We don't waste time getting caught up in our insecurities—we just put on the damn bikini (or the damn Speedo) and get outside. We don't hide out in our hotel room on a Friday night—we go out for drinks with that cute guy from the pool and hook up because time's a wastin'.

We put ourselves out there more, and that's why so many great experiences come our way. If we lived each day like this, we'd open ourselves up to more opportunities and more people.

Experiences and opportunities *do not* always fall into your lap. There's a reason why that go-getter attitude you have on vacation pays off.

5. You'll plan fun dates and explore just like a tourist would.

You, of course, romanticize your new, exotic location when you're away. When you're in a romantic city, it's easier to go on more romantic dates.

In fact, every date on vacation feels like an extra-romantic date, not a regular date. When you go on dates that take place in new and beautiful settings, you're naturally inclined to fall for someone faster. But guess what? You can go on special, unique, and romantic dates back home, too. Regular dates aren't necessary just because you're no longer on vacation! Every city can be romanticized—you just have to date like a tourist and be a tourist in your own city.

6. It's all those positive vibes.

You're on vacation, so of course you're putting out positive vibes and exuding a positive energy. It's that happy, positive energy that men and women find so attractive. There's nothing sexier than a smile, an appreciation for life, confidence, and a carefree attitude.

4

Dating The Right Kind Of People

What we wait around a lifetime for with one person,
we can find in a moment with someone else.
—*Stephanie Klein*

In Chapter 1, you read a comprehensive list of signs you're ready to be with someone. When you read that list and it sounds like you, that's how you know that your next relationship has a good shot of being successful. In Chapter 2, you read about why those who are in great relationships with themselves are the ones most likely to make a relationship with someone else work.

Something equally important, though, is that whoever you start dating also needs to be in a great relationship with himself or herself, and that they, too, can check those boxes from Chapter 1.

For a partnership to work, you *both* have to be fit for a relationship and be ready and available in every way.

When it comes to dating the right kind of people, the very first sign that it's worth pursuing is if **the prospect in question is truly ready for—and wants—a relationship.**

When it comes to dating, it's pretty common to make the same mistake several times before you learn from it. For example, you might have inadvertently dated someone who wasn't over their ex a few times. In other words, your relationship with that person stood no chance because their heart wasn't open and they weren't emotionally available to you. After making that mistake once, twice, or ten times you might start asking the people you date a few more leading questions about where they're at.

You'll know when you've met the right person because it'll be easier than you expected.

If a relationship seems to be going smoothly and everything is easier than you expected, that's a good thing. Why? Because you should never have to win someone over. Winning someone over seems exciting, I know, but it isn't genuine.

Mixed signals do not exist. If someone you're dating seems to be giving you mixed messages, it simply means that they're not relationship material.

If someone you're romantic with leads you to believe that they're into you with their words but their actions prove otherwise, this is not a case of mixed signals. Always pay attention to their actions and watch for consistency. *Actions speak louder than words* is another dating cliché that holds a ton of truth.

If someone you're newly dating says, "I'd love to see you sometime soon" but they never make plans to see you, that's not confusing. That simply means you need to stop wasting your time even thinking about this person because the time you spend putting up with their shit is time you could have given to someone more worthy. A writer named Tim Hoch reminded me that time is my most valuable possession and should only be given to those who deserve it and respect it.

So, how do you know if someone deserves your time and won't waste it? Actions speak louder than words, and if there seems to always be a discrepancy between someone's words and their actions, that's usually a huge red flag and a sign that they'll waste your time.

When someone is really interested in you, you'll know. It'll be clear as day. When it's right, it will feel effortless, natural, and easy. The anxiety sustained from wondering and waiting will be nonexistent. You will hear from this person often and you won't feel confused about how they feel. So don't put up with inconsistency. If someone is inconsistent with you or not treating you right, move on.

Dating the Direct and Honest Type

When it comes to dating, there's always the risk that the person you fall for won't choose you. However, if you're direct, open, and confident while your competition remains passive and elusive, you'll probably be the chosen one.

There's just something so attractive about someone who speaks their mind and fearlessly makes their feelings known.

There are many reasons why we're attracted to direct people. Dating is so much easier when there are no games. We're not interested in putting up with the guessing games that ambiguous and passive types often subject us to.

For example, if we're dating someone who makes us feel unsure of where we stand with them, we'll probably feel compelled to look for someone else. Why? Because we don't want to date anyone who makes us feel uncertain. Uncertainty is one of the worst feelings in the world when it comes to relationships.

Passive men and passive women will cross your path and annoy the f*ck out of you several times before you'll come across someone direct. It'll be a breath of fresh air when it happens.

I'm sure you're guilty of passivity yourself. For example, how many times have you really wanted something from your partner, but worded it as "So I wouldn't mind if..." rather than using language like "I really want" and "It's important to me"?

The inability to be honest and forthcoming is a dating dealbreaker for most people. Many of the men and women who are single and navigating the dating scene read my blog, The Babe Report, and e-mail me with their frustrations regarding how tough dating can be, wanting advice. So, you're probably wondering—what is the most common complaint among singles? It's indirect, confusing people who have no clear intentions and make dating them feel exhausting and stressful instead of fun and fulfilling.

Constantly having to *guess* how someone feels is torture, and I'm not just talking about guessing how they feel about you. It's all the guessing that wears us down. Guessing if they're upset with you about something and guessing if they're lying about something are just some examples of the constant speculation that seems to only happen with certain types of people.

The problem with guesswork is that you not only second-guess the relationship, you also start second-guessing yourself. Plus, guesswork creates unnecessary complications and stress.

The ambiguous types are the way they are for their own reasons. They won't be able to give you the transparency that you need. Direct people are the way they are because they're confident, sure of themselves, and sure of what they want. They likely have checked off most of those boxes from Chapter 1's checklist. They won't cause you anxiety or leave you wondering, waiting and worrying. Instead, they're upfront and assertive which makes the relationship progress smoothly.

I *really* want you guys to understand why you can't date the passive types if you're serious about finding a fulfilling relationship. Just to really drive this point home, here are 7 more reasons why you should date the direct and open type:

1. Dating someone direct won't be stressful or complicated.

Dating should be fun not stressful. When the person you're dating is ambiguous and mysterious, it's complicated instead of easy. It's difficult to trust the ambiguous type, and your confidence level goes down the longer you have to guess how they feel.

When you're dating someone who is open about their feelings for you and showing genuine interest—that's what makes dating enjoyable. Being mindf*cked, however, is not fun. The key is to only date people who bring out the best in you, not the stress in you. Dating uncertainty isn't fun for anyone.

A romantic interest should make you feel secure. Otherwise, your self-esteem is in jeopardy.

2. Direct people exude a sexy confidence.

There's no doubt about it: confidence is sexy as hell. However, it's pretty hard to come across as confident if you're indifferent, indirect, and passive. Confidence stems from being secure with yourself, and secure people are always direct and straightforward with both themselves and others. It takes confidence to be direct, and that's why it's so enticing when you speak up and lay it out on the table.

It's the confident and direct types who really go after what they want. So if you're what they want, they'll actually pursue you. They'll make plans with you in advance, tell you how they feel, and openly discuss all of those uncomfortable "What are we?" and "Are we exclusive?" and "Where is this headed?" topics.

3. Direct types won't waste your time.

The direct type will be upfront and honest if they're not feeling a connection after the first few dates, and they also have no problem being direct about how into you they are if they do feel a connection! Passive types, however, often avoid being honest and have no problem wasting your time if it means they can side-step an uncomfortable conversation.

Direct types aren't afraid of uncomfortable conversations—they simply believe in honesty. Even if they do find certain topics to be uncomfortable, they understand the value of being straightforward in relationships. The beauty of being direct is that your partner can feel confident knowing that if something is bothering you, you'll at least talk about it, which puts an over-thinking mind at ease.

When your partner is direct they're easier to trust, and there are fewer things to potentially misinterpret throughout your relationship. When someone seems hard to read instead of direct, it's often because they're not all in and they're avoiding being honest for that reason. This is exactly why ambiguity is so frustrating when it comes to dating.

4. Direct people make you feel at ease.

When there is less reason to doubt the person you are with, there is less stress associated with the relationship. We need less stress in our lives, not more, so you must walk away from anyone who is making you second-guess yourself.

5. Being direct shows strength of character.

It takes a person of good character to be forthcoming about their intentions instead of passive or nonchalant. If they're direct, that's them being real.

Another great thing about dating direct people is that they're refreshingly honest about their intentions and clear about what motivates them in a relationship.

6. Transparency is key in relationships.

In dating, you can't beat around the bush due to fear of rejection or due to the fear of an adverse reaction. A transparent person will communicate their emotions and be honest about how they're feeling—and what they're thinking.

Nicole Prause, Ph.D. and Sexual Psychophysiologist, pointed out to me that:

Some people really struggle to communicate their emotions. Desiring somebody 'direct' is actually code for wanting someone who is aware of their own emotions and can accurately communicate them, but also relieves some of the stress on the partner who is trying to accurately understand their emotions. When any part of this complex chain breaks down, it can be a source of conflict and can be central to the relationship ending. The majority of men and women want an emotionally intelligent and communicative partner!

Emotional transparency is also what helps you feel like they're all in and not half there. It is key in relationships because it allows for closeness and causes the relationship to progress rather than fall apart.

7. Communicating directly demonstrates effort.

By taking the time to communicate directly, your partner is putting in the effort. In some ways, we're a reflection of our partners because the way they treat us is reflected in our general aura. If they put in the effort and treat us like we're special, that is emulated and mirrored in our self-worth. So if we have a partner who is lazy, passive, and doesn't bother to communicate their feelings with us, that will damage our self-esteem and could ruin all the hard work you've put into loving yourself.

Now, let's dive into a few more things you should look for when it comes to dating the right kind of people:

Date Someone Who Asks You Questions

Date someone who has standards and asks you real questions. Someone who has standards will ask a lot of questions to figure out who you are, and that's a great thing. It's a sign that they're searching for something meaningful.

If they're asking questions, it means they're serious about a potential relationship with you, and this is a sign that they have high self-worth and high standards. Someone with low self-worth and no standards won't typically ask very many questions.

Not only are questions a great indicator of how serious someone is about you, but they're also a fantastic way to keep conversations stimulating, intriguing and engaging. There's nothing worse than dating someone who is boring to talk to. Asking and answering some real and hard-hitting questions are great ways to keep your exchanges interesting.

Date Someone Who Prioritizes You

There's no worse feeling than feeling undervalued by someone you're in a relationship with. In the beginning stages of dating, take note of whether or not he or she is prioritizing you. When it comes to prioritizing you, the beginning sets the tone for the course of the relationship. You'll know when someone is prioritizing you when they're giving you their Saturday nights, including you in their existing plans, and making plans with you on a regular basis.

Date Someone Who You're in the Moment With

So many of us suffer from anxiety or inadvertently have our guard up sometimes. It's a common problem to go through the motions rather than feeling emotions sometimes, and it can be tough (for all of us) to truly enjoy a moment *while it's happening*. The ability to be in-the-moment on a date isn't overrated—it's essential.

I know that I personally have always had problems cruising through life without anything imprinting. My body might be there on a date, but I'm not really present. Maybe that's not a bad thing since I really do *notice* if a guy I'm dating forces me to be in the moment and that moment actually imprints.

People who care about you will notice when you're not engaged in the moment. They'll notice your lack of eye contact and they'll notice when you fail to laugh at one of their jokes because you weren't really listening.

It takes a special type of person to be able to force you to be in the moment. How this person accomplishes this is sort of unexplainable. They just somehow bring you into the moment, and it honestly just requires a genuine connection. That's what we need in a partner.

Find Someone Who Plans Grand Gestures

Grand gestures, in my opinion, separate the boys from the men and the girls from the women. A grand gesture can be as easy as directly communicating your feelings, planning a surprise date night or organizing a weekend getaway. These gestures make a relationship go from mediocre to totally awesome—and who wants to be in a mediocre relationship?

See, it's easy to call and say, "Congratulations on landing that big new client!" But couples should celebrate each other, and that means taking you out to celebrate or planning some sort of nice surprise.

In this lazy, entitled, and passive dating culture, a grand gesture is kind of remarkable. When someone takes initiative and actually plans something romantic for the two of you to do together, big or small, it's the thought that counts and it's the thought that makes it a gesture.

I personally think an open conversation is a grand gesture, too. It takes guts for someone to lay their feelings on the line, and it's not always easy to do it.

Date Someone Who You Can Do Nothing With and Everything With

The best relationships are the ones where you enjoy yourself when you're doing absolutely nothing. You simply love spending time with each other. (It helps if you make each other laugh!) And yet, you both still have a strong desire to do fun, unique activities together as well. That means that as a couple, you're well-rounded.

A couple who only goes on regular dates together or only wants to "Netflix and Chill" will bond much less than a couple who sometimes goes on extravagant, unique, and special dates together.

By planning special date nights that stray from the mediocre and are instead memorable, exciting, and special, you're building a much stronger bond and creating memories that shine as constant reminders of how great you are together.

This is the type of date that promotes a special connection and generates that spell-binding chemistry. If things are going well with someone you're dating, it's these types of dates that will keep the momentum going.

It's these experiences that leave a lasting impression and allow you to stand out from your competition. You'll stand out because the date is dying, and you're someone who is trying to bring it back.

In other words, the best way to form a genuine connection with someone is to create memories based on exceptional real life experiences that you've shared together.

You don't need tips on how to do 'nothing' together, so here are some ideas of memorable dates that will bring you closer together and enhance your relationship:

The date that gets you out of your comfort zone. Hypothetically speaking, let's say one of your biggest fears is getting up on stage and singing karaoke. If your date encourages you to do this and reminds you that it's simply a room full of strangers you'll never have to see again, that's an awesome date. You have to admit: whenever you do something that falls outside of your comfort zone, you always feel really good after. It's a different kind of feeling and a different kind of date. And guess what? Different is good—because it's memorable.

The date where you get wined and dined the *fancy* way. I love taco Tuesday as much as the next gal, but there's something to be said about getting wined and dined at a nicer restaurant sometimes. That type of date stands out. The ambiance is romantic, and you're also being given an opportunity to get dressed up and smell nice. Dinner at a nice restaurant is a traditional date, one that is surprisingly dying out. Bring it back and see how far it gets you.

A date that gets you out of the city. A mini road trip or a weekend getaway can make for a fantastic date. Just go for a drive, get out of the city, and experience something new. It'll feel like you went on a mini vacation and you'll be able to talk and get to know each other during the car ride. Make sure you get along during your first date, then plan an adventurous getaway together.

A date that gets you out on the water. Going on a dinner cruise, a sunset cruise, a sailboat ride, or taking a little ferry adventure is a great date. Most people love getting out on the water, seeing beautiful scenery, and feeling the fresh breeze—it's just hands down an incredible date idea.

The date that gets your adrenaline pumping. If you're a little afraid of heights, push yourself to do a ropes course, a zipline adventure, or a helicopter tour. Any date that gets your adrenaline pumping will create a bonding experience and remind you how fun dating can be. Your thirst for adventure likely isn't quenched very often which is why adventurous excursions are fantastic dates.

The cultural date. It's not often enough that we go see a play inspired by the 1920s or go to an art exhibit. Cultural dates like these are great because you're being entertained and discovering culture which feels more like an event than a hang-out. Anything that feels like a real outing is what a 'date' should be.

The date where you're immersed in nature. Studies have shown that spending time in nature is linked to happiness, so you're bound to feel good during an outdoorsy date. Go on a beautiful, scenic hike and enjoy the view at the top with a picnic. Grab a few blankets and go star-gazing. Being outdoors is good for you, and a walk or hike outside allows for plenty of time for you and your date to talk and get to know each other. Not only that, but exercise gets those endorphins pumping which contributes to those feel-good vibes on your date.

The date where you learn something new. Any date where you get to learn something together is unique and exciting. Think dance classes, walking tours, cooking classes, painting nights, seminars, etc. A date should never be boring or mundane. A date shouldn't always be a boring or mundane activity that you'd typically do which is why enrolling in a class for your date is perfect.

The date where you watch the sunset. We don't watch the sunset often enough. It sounds silly, but it kind of requires planning. You have to pick a beautiful location or a cool rooftop that offers a great view of the sunset and plan to go at the right time so you don't miss it. Bring a bottle of wine and watch the sun go down together. It's the epitome of romance.

A date where you laugh your ass off. When you go see improv comedy or stand-up comedy, you're both going to be laughing lots and seeing a fun side of each other. These types of dates allow you to loosen up and enjoy stress-free live entertainment. It can be significantly more fun than sitting across from each other at a bar.

A date that brings out your inner child. It's fun to go to a playground and have your date push you on the swings, go to an extreme indoor play park, or build a giant sandcastle on the beach. We all have a little kid somewhere inside us, just begging for an excuse to come out.

A date that doesn't involve alcohol. When you cut alcohol out of the equation, you're forced to get creative with your date ideas. You can play board games together, go for a nice walk, or get ice cream at that cool spot you keep reading about. It's fun to get to know each other on a deeper level while sober and clear-headed. Plus, if you can't have fun with someone when you're sober, that means you're dating the wrong person.

Anyone Who Says "Maybe" A Lot Probably Won't Make a Good Partner

Remember how important I said it was to date someone direct? Well anyone who uses the word "maybe" a lot is probably more of a passive type.

If you've been single for a significant period of time, you're probably smart enough not to settle for less than what you deserve. That being said, I hope you know to watch out for anyone who says "maybe" a lot.

The "M" word is complete BS. You don't have time for maybe. You need a "yes," and you shouldn't settle for less.

For example, if someone throws you a, "Maybe I can see you this weekend, I'll let you know," or, "Maybe I'd be looking for something serious down the road," you should consider that a waste of your time and a clear indication that your value isn't being recognized.

If they're saying maybe to you, they're pretty much saying

no. People who often say maybe tend to be passive, noncommittal, and elusive, not to mention confusing as hell. None of those qualities are attractive in a man or in a woman.

While girls and boys often put up with these indirect guessing games and mixed signals, most women and men won't.

> *Being single doesn't mean you're weak.*
> *It means you're strong enough*
> *to wait for what you deserve.*
> —*Niall Horan*

Part of the reason for this newfound intolerance of the word "maybe" is the fact that grown men and women who have their lives in order want partners who are as sure about them as they are about themselves.

If uttering the word "yes" is too much of a commitment for someone, then chances are they won't be very good at committing in general.

By refusing to give direct, set answers, they'll make one hell of a complicated, frustrating, and confusing partner.

Mark Manson's viral article, "Fuck Yes Or No," is a great testament to this theory. It sums up the concept that there is not—and there never should be—any in-between or gray area in a healthy relationship. His theory is that if it's not a "fuck yes" it most certainly is a "no" because there shouldn't be any such thing as "maybe" in a functioning relationship.

In many ways, by saying "maybe," one is showing weakness and being noncommittal. It's a form of cowardice which is why many people with deep-seated insecurities say "maybe" all the time.

You might not realize how sexy a "yes" man or a "yes" woman is until you actually date one, which is why you should hold out for this type of person.

It's nice to date someone who doesn't complicate your relationship or add stress to your life with "maybe" this and "maybe" that.

Remember, everything is just easy with direct people.

Perfection is Boring

Why you should date someone with flaws.

> *Perfect is overrated. Perfect is boring.*
> —*Tina Fey*

We have all met the 'perfect' type: The uncomplicated ones who don't seem to have any major quirks or troubles. They cruise through life effortlessly, and it is rare that anything can stress them out enough to break a sweat.

You'll never catch these types in a bad mood, and you'll never be able to snap a bad photo of them. The perfect type is somehow always dressed and styled impeccably. It's as though they have never slept through their alarm or rolled out of bed and been forced to go out in public with unwashed hair. Instead, they always look perfect. Everything about them is ideal.

Then there is the 'imperfect' type. The ones who often get all of the bad luck. It's not easy for them to stick to their New Year's Resolutions, but they'll sure as hell try. They sleep through their alarm, rarely look polished, and they march to the beat of their own drum. They're the quirky type who have unconventional thought patterns, anxiety, and troubles. But they persevere through it all. The way the imperfect type does things is atypical, to say the least. They take each experience as it comes and learn from their failures. They find a way around the roadblocks and write down new goals and celebrate their achievements. They might not seem as easy to date as the perfect type, but they are not without their perks. Here are some reasons why you should be open to dating someone imperfect:

Perfection is too predictable. Perfection is simple and easy, but it's too predictable. There will not be as many surprises or interesting anecdotes when dating someone perfect as there would be with someone imperfect. It is unlikely that you view yourself as a vision of perfection, so why would you want to be with someone perfect? Unpredictable situations are what keeps us young and what keeps us from getting bored. The quirks that come with an imperfect person are perfect for those who are tired of the same pattern and the same routine.

They'll have amazing stories. Their stories will not bore you. In fact, you'll likely learn something from their unique stories. They will tell tales about some interesting, unorthodox way they went about getting something they wanted. Perhaps their stories will be about their failures and hardships and what they took from those experiences. Maybe something hilarious happened to them because they did the wrong thing or got in some sort of trouble by breaking the rules. Imperfections give people character and that's how they get the best stories to tell.

Imperfection translates into depth of character. Someone imperfect has likely been through a lot in life since things don't happen easily for them. What they want out of life doesn't come effortlessly—they have to put all their energy into something if they want it to work out—and it often still doesn't. They are therefore raw, real, resilient, and complex. They have depth and strength of character. They have failed too many times to count and it makes them stronger and more enlightened each time.

They keep you on your toes. Going back to unpredictability, that's what keeps you on your toes. Routines and schedules often followed by perfectionists do nothing but bore you. The anticipation that anything could happen makes life exciting, and if you date someone who's up for anything, you'll always have that excitement. The imperfect types live their lives this way because they are not crippled by the fear of failure and are more likely to take risks. They don't mind if they embarrass themselves and they try not to care too much about who judges them or what others think.

They will encourage your adventurous side to come out. The simple, perfect, and boring life rarely comes with a ton of adventure. It's the stressed out and anxious people who seek adventure to distract themselves from their troubles. Rest assured, they will bring out your adventurous side. They seek out positivity so as to not be dragged down by negative situations. They know how to take a break from their worries in a fun and spontaneous way. They don't need to plan every trip down to the last detail—they aren't perfectionists. They go with the flow.

They won't judge you for your imperfections. They don't care if you have flaws because they have flaws, too. Each time you do something quirky, unconventional, or 'flawed' they see a bit of themselves in you and smile. Your oddball traits don't bother them as long as you have goals and you generally have your shit together. As long as you're working towards something and you have ambition, plans, and dreams, they will never be bothered by your imperfections.

How to Attract the Right Kind of People

So now that you know what kind of people you should be dating, you probably want to know how to attract these people.

In Chapter 6, we're going to talk about rejection attachments which can be part of the reason why women consistently pick the wrong men (and why men pick the wrong women). The attachment to rejection and familiarity with failure causes us to pick partners who we instinctually *know* it won't work out with.

This pattern can change once you're conscious of it, and once you begin to take steps to attract the right kind of people. Here are some points to remember if you want to attract the right partner:

- If you want to attract someone who isn't afraid of commitment, you have to be brave enough to verbalize what you're looking for, effectively weeding out those who aren't looking or anything serious.
- If you learn to practice gratitude and you have a positive outlook on life, you'll attract someone positive, and it'll be less likely that negativity will be present in the relationship.
- By mastering healthy habits *before* you enter into a

new relationship, you won't have to pretend to be something you're not once you're in a relationship.

- If you truly love yourself, you'll attract the right kind of people. If you exude confidence, your partner will be confident in the relationship.

5

Understanding What You Want And Need In A Partner

> *Some day, someone will walk into your life*
> *and make you realize why it never worked out*
> *with anyone else.*
> *—Anonymous*

Every time a relationship or an 'almost-relationship' didn't work out, you learned something. You learned what qualities that person was missing, and you taught yourself more about what you really need and want in a partner. Hopefully, something you learned is that physical attraction is not going to keep a relationship afloat.

There's Much More to a Relationship than Chemistry and Physical Attraction

A common mistake we make when selecting a partner is focusing solely on who we have an intense chemistry with and putting those we feel physically attracted to or lustful towards on a pedestal.

In other words, just dating all the hot people is a big no-no.

Although the chemistry, the connection, and the attraction are all integral to a relationship, you shouldn't settle for someone who doesn't treat you right simply because those three ingredients are present.

Remember that ultimately, you want to find *love* not *lust*.

You can't disregard someone's bad behavior just because the chemistry or sex is great—or just because they're smoking hot. If you know that you aren't satisfied with the way they treat you, then deep down you know that a relationship with them probably won't work long-term—even if the attraction is fierce.

Keep in mind that it's possible to be attracted to someone who has an enticing personality but who is below your standards looks-wise. If you give it a chance, you'll find yourself attracted to people who aren't anywhere near a 10/10 physically. You'll notice that it's extremely common to be sexually attracted to someone based solely off of their personality and demeanor. So if you think that you need to date models in order to summon your sexual urges, think again.

If you find that you're still pretty shallow when you choose your partners, and you notice that you're pursuing people based on looks or sex, you might not be ready for a meaningful relationship yet. Eventually, when diving into the shallow end of the pool results in nothing but bruises and scrapes, you'll be ready to test the waters of the deep end, and that is where you'll find something extraordinary.

If you have trouble with being too focused on the physical, try this: Write down the top 10 qualities that you would look for in a significant other, aside from physical attraction. Choose the qualities that you'd need them to have in order for there to be any chance at something long-lasting. You'll find that the simple act of writing out this list of desired traits can be quite powerful in reminding you that the person you're with needs to offer more than just physical appeal.

What Can Friendships with the Opposite Sex Teach You about Relationships?

If you find that you're always pursuing relationships solely based on physical attraction and you're stubborn when it comes to dating outside of your "type," you might not be dating the right people.

You may need to foster more friendships with the opposite sex in order to figure out what you want in a significant other besides physical attraction.

Not all of you have friends of the opposite gender, but all of you should, because it's these friendships that can teach you a lot about what type of romantic relationship you ultimately want.

By seeking out friendships with the opposite sex, you're teaching yourself that there is more to a romantic connection than the physical. When you spend time with friends of the opposite gender, you'll learn that it is possible to feel those romantic feelings for someone who is not your type physically.

Think about it this way: when you choose friends of the opposite sex, you're not typically choosing them based on how attractive they are. You're choosing them based on personality—and they're often the *opposite* of what you consider physically attractive. However, the more time you spend with them, the more likely it is that a flicker of desire or some sort of romantic inclination towards them will cross your mind. If you put some thought into what it is about them that you find attractive (since it's not their outward appearance) you'll have learned something important: you'll have learned what *qualities* you find attractive in the opposite sex.

Discovering what you want in a partner can even stem from the time you spend with your friends' partners. You'll end up learning a lot about what you seek in a partner based on the traits of theirs that you perceive and admire. You spend time with them, since they're dating your friends, right? And while physically-speaking they might not be your type, they might sometimes seem attractive to you when you observe them.

Why Failed Relationships are so Valuable

If you're perpetually single or you have a lot of breakup stories, you're not a sob story. What I mean is, when you recognize how valuable a breakup is, you won't think of your relationship failures as failures anymore.

Breakups are the most valuable dating lessons you can get your hands on. If you're lucky, your ex will be willing to tell you what he liked and didn't like. Even if your ex isn't the type to give feedback, you can still self-reflect to figure out what mistakes were made, what was missing on both sides, and what you can take from the failed relationship.

Someone who has gone through a series of breakups, plenty of heartbreak, and tons of failed attempts at love has now gained priceless knowledge, insight, and understanding of how relationships work. Instead of ending up with the wrong person, you got the chance (again and again) to check in with your needs and decide what you really want. Over and over, you were pushed to self-reflect and work on bettering yourself while reminding yourself of what it is you really seek in a partner.

You developed a thick skin and an appreciation for real talk. You stopped needing a partner and started fulfilling your own needs.

Your failed relationships have molded you, polished you, and prepped you so that when you meet the right person, you'll be ready.

6

What Have You Been Doing Wrong? 10 Big Mistakes You're Making

We accept the love we think we deserve.
—Stephen Chbosky

Have you noticed a pattern in your relationships that you're not proud of? Would you consider most of your past relationships cringe-worthy attempts rather than successes? If you have a tough time keeping prospects interested, you might begin to believe that you're simply not good enough for anyone. That couldn't be farther from the truth.

In the next chapter, we'll discuss one of the biggest mistakes people make in dating which is dating unavailable people. There are, however, several other dating mistakes you should become conscious of before you begin a new relationship.

Chances are that the rejection and failed relationships you've experienced in the past have caused you to put up walls and anticipate failure. If you expect to fail, you subconsciously identify yourself with unsuccessful relationships.

> *You will have bad times,*
> *but they will always wake you up*
> *to recognize the stuff you weren't paying attention to.*
> —Robin Williams

There are some common mistakes you've been making that may have caused you to lose out on love. You could easily be your own solution as soon as you're aware of what you've been doing wrong. Here are 10 relationship mistakes you may be guilty of that very well could be the reason why it's not working out for you romantically:

1. You're self-sabotaging potential relationships due to an attachment to rejection.

If you're used to being rejected and disregarded, you might unconsciously seek out rejection because it's what you're familiar with. If you're seeking rejection without realizing it, you could have a psychological attachment to rejection.

When you identify yourself with disappointment, disapproval, and rejection, you can develop what's known as a rejection attachment. Some of you are guilty of ignoring those who are interested in you and instead, you're going after people who don't seem to be that interested. Perhaps this is proof of a rejection attachment. You know you'll likely get turned down since the people you're pursuing aren't showing any signs of approval or interest towards you. But since rejection is what you know, you're alright with it. The rejection is familiar territory, and it's weirdly comfortable.

Mike Bundrant, a life coach, retired psychotherapist, and co-founder of iNLP Center, said in his article on psychological attachments:

> *Seeking approval from someone who will never approve is the same as seeking rejection... It's like an autopilot that was set in the wrong direction. It just keeps going there. You don't like the destination but can't figure out how to reprogram it.*

People who have a rejection attachment probably believe that they are undesirable, so they collect evidence that supports that belief. This evidence-gathering would, of course, include seeking out approval from those who aren't willing to give them any sort of validation and pursuing those who aren't fully returning their affections.

Word to the wise: don't pursue someone who doesn't want a relationship or someone who doesn't want you.

2. Your attitude towards dating is generally quite negative.

If you've had way too many horrible dating experiences to count, it can be tough to be optimistic about dating. Perhaps you've been dumped, cheated on, rejected, left for somebody 'better,' and told you weren't good enough so many times that you now have a negative attitude towards dating.

The problem with not being positive is that you won't attract anything positive. You get what you give, so if you're giving off a negative attitude when it comes to all things dating related, it'll be noticed—even if it's subtle or subconscious.

The law of attraction rightfully suggests that any limiting beliefs towards dating or love are stopping you from attracting a mate. If you believe that you're not good enough to be adored by someone, you will never be adored by someone. If you believe that you'll be rejected, you'll be rejected. Anytime you catch yourself thinking these negative beliefs, make sure to challenge them because negativity is a bad habit that needs to be broken.

3. You have low self-esteem.

You have low self-esteem from being rejected, but guess what? You're being rejected *because* of your low self-esteem. This cycle is proof that your low self-esteem can cause a relationship to fail.

Men are not attracted to women with low self-esteem and no self-confidence, and women are not attracted to men who lack those qualities, either. Confidence and self-love are attractive qualities, and that's the number one thing you need to work on if you want to find love.

If you don't think you're a total catch, why would someone else think you are?

4. You don't know what you want.

The girl with a hot body is a bimbo, and the smart girl is boring. The funny guy is a player, but the nice guy has no sense of humor. You can't have it all; no one is perfect.

Again, make that list of the top ten things you look for in a partner. Put things into perspective of what is *really* important and stop writing people off so easily.

If you seek a partner solely based on looks, it'll be much less likely that you'll find a meaningful and lasting partnership.

5. You're always distracted by other options.

Part of your problem could be that you tend to keep your options open, so you keep your nets in the water and keep prospects on the backburner.

Perhaps it boosts your ego knowing you've got options and prospects on the bench. However, keeping them in these nets does nothing for you because you aren't truly giving any of them a chance, and they know it—which means it won't work out with any of them.

If you meet someone great and you jump in with both feet, you could miss out on some other options.

So what? You can't live your life being 'afraid' of what you're missing out on. Everyone has other options, but not everyone who is in a relationship thinks that they're missing out on something else. It's unlikely that these other options are better than the person you have in your sights—because you were obviously drawn to this person in the first place for a reason. We'll get into a more in-depth discussion of this problem in Chapter 7.

6. You're either too needy or too independent.

Nobody enjoys either extreme. Being too needy is terrible because nobody likes feeling as though you're relying on them too much. It can be overwhelming for your partner to think that they're fully responsible for your happiness because you 'need' and rely on him or her too much.

However, your partner, of course, wants to be needed a little bit. They won't want you to be so independent that you care way too little, and aren't affected by anything.

7. You're not using the law of averages to your advantage.

In Chapter 1, we discussed which signs prove that you might be ready for a relationship. If you're ready, that's great, but a relationship won't fall in your lap. You have to go out and meet people.

In other words, you're probably not putting yourself out there enough—not by a mile. If you've been rejected a bunch of times and you've developed a fear of rejection, you might be avoiding the dating world altogether.

The law of averages indicates that the more "no"s you experience, the closer you'll get to a "yes." It's the magic of probability. In other words, the more dates you go on that don't work out, or the more times you're rejected, the closer you are to finding someone that it does work out with.

If you don't put yourself out there, you'll remain far away from that coveted "yes." Mr. or Mrs. Right isn't going to come knocking on your door while you're watching Netflix, asking you if it's possible to borrow a cup of sugar. Nobody does that anymore. Sorry, but you'll actually have to go out, meet people, try something new, and be open to dating those who might not be your typical type. Just be open and out there, stop hiding, and it'll happen.

8. You don't have high enough standards.

You should have high standards for how you deserve to be treated. For example, if he or she blows off plans with you, you can't be too nice about it. If you're too nice, people will walk all over you instead of trying to be better for you. If they think they can get away with treating you badly, they'll keep pushing boundaries to see what they can get away with.

9. You're complacent.

Instead of asking for the things you deserve, you settle for what you're given. Perhaps you're content with the way things are, but maybe that means you're too easy going in relationships. Don't give the milk away for free—if you're not happy about something, speak up, because the best relationships are the ones where both people are happy. You should still pick your battles (don't bitch about everything) but the right person will respect you for standing up for what you deserve as it shows you have self-respect.

10. You're picking the wrong partners and dating unavailable people.

Don't chase after someone who doesn't seem all that into you or someone who doesn't want anything serious. It'll never end well.

One of the biggest dating mistakes you can make is dating people who want completely different things than you—especially when it comes to how serious they want the relationship to be.

Even more importantly, don't pursue anyone who has someone else in the picture. Before you pursue someone, find out how single he or she really is. If they're not over their ex, they're very recently single, or whoever they really wanted has turned them down, it's best to not bother. Avoid people who have others taking up too much of their limited emotional real estate. In the next chapter, we'll discuss in more detail why you can't date unavailable people and what an 'unavailable' person actually means.

7

Dating Unavailable People

I used to think that the worst thing in life was
to end up alone. It's not.
The worst thing in life is to end up
with people that make you feel alone.
—Robin Williams

This book is all about helping you stock up on the advice you need in your back pocket *before* you start dating again. It's about knowing you finally want a relationship and collecting valuable relationship advice to help you find success in love this time around. That's why there's an entire chapter dedicated to the importance of dating available people.

Dating someone who is emotionally and mentally unavailable will make you feel even lonelier than you would feel if you were alone.

This chapter is meant to help you figure out whether or not you're truly available to be in a relationship *and* to help you decipher if your prospect is available or unavailable.

Unavailable People Have the Wrong Intent

Intent is fundamental to any relationship. Emotionally unavailable people don't actually intend on the relationship getting serious. What you want is to meet someone whose intent is to get serious, develop a real connection, and move forward. Find out what someone's intentions are *before* you invest too much of your time. All you have to do is ask.

Someone who is chronically distracted by other options is unavailable and therefore not relationship material.

Being single in the digital age, we have options—*lots* of options. Although we're lucky to have access to hundreds of singles on dating apps and at bars, there's a pretty serious issue that comes with this: too many options.

Too much choice is ruining dating, and if you can't date unavailable people, that means you can't date anyone who is chronically distracted by other options.

Think about it: the popularity of dating apps provide us with effortless access to all of these choices, leaving us with plenty of opportunities at our fingertips. This, however, is not always a good thing and can lead to dating stagnation if you don't become aware of the paradox.

Having too many options can certainly be overwhelming and prevent you from giving up the single life. You could get overwhelmed by the options and suddenly feel paralyzed, not acting on any of them. Even worse, you could end up alone because the deceptive perception of something better *always* being around the corner can cause you to never just choose someone and stop looking. Perhaps this is why some of us are so picky. It's likely we will take for granted an amazing catch—someone special who we meet and discard.

If you meet someone special, how likely are you to stop using online dating sites altogether and just focus on that one person? What sometimes happens is that no matter how much you like the person you're dating, you'll still chat with others and explore other options. When you always think someone better is right around the corner, you're allowing yourself to get distracted from the amazing person right in front of you. It's your call, but just know that your inability to focus on him or her could completely screw things up for you. If you can break this habit and try dating one person at a time, that's you giving it a real shot.

The Paradox of Choice Can Make Dating Seem Hopeless

The paradox of choice has the ability to cause you to hesitate instead of committing because you're reluctant to give up your other options. But what if these better options are a mere illusion, and giving them up is the path to happiness and fulfillment?

Imagining that you have a ton of amazing options to choose from makes it difficult to choose, so you choose no one—and that's getting you nowhere and typifying you as unavailable.

The paradox of choice causes single men and women to feel lonely even while surrounded by options because they have trouble choosing when there is so much choice. This could be why so many of us inadvertently choose to remain single, neglecting promising opportunities that present themselves.

The privilege of being able to choose may be more detrimental to your dating life than it is advantageous.

If you do decide that you want a meaningful relationship, you have to give up your other options, and it's not as scary as you think to do so:

Being picky and entitled won't get you anywhere. It's not simply a matter of singles being hesitant, picky, or indecisive. Yes, if you happen to be seeing more than one person who you have feelings for, indecisiveness comes into play. However, other problems include narrow-mindedness, greed, and a sense of entitlement.

The issue is not that you are too choosy; the issue is that there is too much choice—choice that you may be tempted to indulge in often, whether it's because you can't bring yourself to delete that dating app or you can't help but be interested in someone else even if you're already dating someone amazing.

It is choice that causes you to be *extremely* picky, and it is choice that causes your narrow-mindedness. It's common to also feel entitled to something or someone better because of your awareness of your city's options.

The privilege of choice causes ridiculously high expectations. The more options we have the privilege to choose from, the pickier you become. Someone has to *really* stand out among all of those options to get our attention. Our expectations are too high. If you keep second-guessing whether or not a man or woman is right for you, you'll lose out on scoring someone amazing.

Instead of having high expectations, we should focus on the root of relationships: the feeling you get when you're with someone special. Focus on how someone makes you feel, rather than focusing on whether or not they live up to your expectations.

Dating uncertainty is caused by too much choice. Having too much choice makes us second-guess ourselves and makes us second-guess the person we're with, which could be one of the reasons why you're still single.

Having options can be quite confusing. It is common to feel uncertain when you start to get serious with someone because you start to second-guess whether or not he or she is the right one. It's easy to think "the right one is still out there" when dating apps are constantly reminding you just how many really *are* still out there. It is a modern-day dating dilemma.

While many people agree that in general, too much choice can complicate life, one of the biggest believers in this theory is Dr. David Schwartz. In 2004, he wrote an influential book entitled *The Paradox of Choice: Why More Is Less* in which he points out that having so much choice causes us to be unsatisfied with any one choice.

The feeling of uncertainty when you're dating someone great but you aren't sure how you feel is a common problem. It is caused by us feeling unsatisfied with a prospect because we're sure we'd be settling, and we're sure we could do better—but if what if we're wrong? The more choices we have, the less content we will be with someone, no matter how great he or she is—unless we stop letting those choices distract us and instead focus on who is in front of us.

The hookup culture is caused by the plethora of options. The hookup culture is thriving. Meanwhile, real relationships are few and far between. What happened? Casual hookups are a dime a dozen, but what about meaningful relationships that leave you feeling fulfilled and at peace instead of empty, anxious, and alone? Having a plethora of options is tempting us to participate solely in the hookup culture instead of being content with one person—no matter how wonderful he or she is.

While hooking up is fun—and easy due to our accessibility to singles via dating apps—it's not getting us where we want to be. It's not getting us closer to finding love.

Earlier generations were not as distracted by options. Our parents' generation found it much simpler to choose a partner. There were no dating apps available to them, and they were not provided with a plethora of options. When they met someone special, they held on to that person. The choice was easy to be with that person because there were not a lot of options to begin with and no distractions complicating their relationships.

Online dating has tremendous advantages, but our parents didn't have online dating and they were blissfully ignorant to who else was available to them. Granted, they may not have had as easy a time meeting someone, but this made their dating decisions much easier.

How to overcome dating difficulties caused by too much choice:

If the amount of choice you have is causing you to feel uncertain about someone you are dating, ask yourself: is this person a good catch? How sure are you that you could do better than this person? Have you given this person a real chance, and have you genuinely gotten to know them yet? Is your desire to check out other options simply due to an irrational fear of missing out?

The solution is to forget about the fact that you have other options and focus on the prospect in question for awhile, just to be sure.

If you put your other options out of your mind and spend some quality time with one person, the results will likely be quite positive. Your feelings for them will grow, especially if during that time you are not distracted by other options. For example, if you used a dating app to meet someone, that's great—but delete that dating app once you've met someone with whom you feel a connection, especially if you feel that they possess the qualities you are looking for.

If you feel something with this person, it's worth exploring. But you can't really explore anything if you're distracted by other options.

A good catch isn't as common to find as you might think. It may take self-discipline to see where things go with one person rather than continue looking, but the rewards of a fulfilling relationship with someone special are well worth sacrificing other choices. Until you realize this, you'll be dubbed 'unavailable.'

Emotionally unavailable people are often emotionally immature.

Sometimes, the reason someone isn't emotionally available is because they're not emotionally mature. It's much more common for girls and boys to be unavailable than it is for men and women to be unavailable. Here are 10 signs your prospect has the maturity needed to be in a relationship:

1. They're committed to a healthy lifestyle. When they're committed to things like their health, their physical fitness, the cleanliness of their apartment, paying their bills on time, and their side hustle, this shows that they have roots.

2. They make plans and they aren't passive or lazy. Your boy or your girl might casually suggest you go out for a nice dinner sometime soon, but your man or woman will actually make plans and tell you that they've made reservations for 7:00 Friday evening at that new Italian spot that got rave reviews. You won't have to worry passivity, laziness, or minimal effort if you're dating someone who can adult.

3. They'll be straightforward and communicate. A real man or woman will be straightforward instead of beating around the bush. (You read all about the importance of dating the direct type in Chapter 4.)

4. They have follow-through and their words match up with their actions. If they say they'll be somewhere, they really will be there. If they say they want to see you, they always follow up with a plan. They are reliable, not flaky.

5. They have ambitious plans and goals for the future. They not only know what they want to achieve in life, but they also have plans on how to achieve those goals. They live life with purpose and drive.

6. They're picky. They're picky because they can be. They have standards because they know their worth.

7. They have passions and hobbies. They have something in their life that they're incredibly passionate about and interests that have nothing to do with you.

8. They won't bend over backward for you. A real man or a real woman won't always be available or accommodating. They won't bend over backward for you or be at your beck and call.

9. They don't need constant reassurance or validation. They have self-confidence and they don't require validation from others. (You read all about this in Chapter 2).

10. They're adventurous. The same old routine bores them because they're not simple-minded. They want to experience new things and keep it interesting.

When You Date Someone Who is Thinking about Someone Else

Another reason a prospect isn't available to you is because they're too busy thinking about someone else. When you date someone who is thinking about someone else you're setting yourself up for failure.

It's extremely difficult to get someone to commit to you if there's someone else they're thinking about. If you're honestly looking for something real, make sure that whoever you start a relationship with is single, unattached and available in every way. Ask around, ask them, pay attention to the signs, and know their dating history.

When you meet someone who's available in every sense of the word, you'll know. You can sense these things. This goes back to the concept of your intuition guiding you. Find someone who hasn't thought about their ex, or anyone else, for a long, long time. You want a partnership with someone who has nobody else on their mind, distracting them from you. Seek those who are open to a relationship, healthy, and happy.

Every single one of us has a limited amount of emotional real estate available for loving and caring for someone. Nobody wants to be with someone who has an even more limited amount of room due to consuming thoughts of 'the one that got away.'

Some people who aren't over their ex or have someone else in mind who they'd rather be with are going to lie to you.

They won't want you to know that there's someone else in their thoughts because they know that you won't be happy if you find out. That's why sometimes you'll have to figure it out for yourself. Here are 5 red flags:

1. It was a recent breakup.
2. The breakup wasn't their decision.
3. They talk about their ex.
4. They compare you to their ex.
5. They were recently into someone who didn't reciprocate their feelings.

For a relationship to be rewarding, satisfying and worth your while, both parties need to absolutely *adore* each other.

How is it possible to fall head over heels for someone when part of your heart is with someone else?

Here are 5 signs that your love interest has moved on from any old flames:

1. It's been at least one year since their last love interest.
2. There is no electronic footprint left (no social media connection, no texts, no photos).
3. Old habits have died hard (they don't insist on going to the same places and doing the same things that they did with their ex).
4. They don't bring up their ex or make comparisons.
5. They have healthy boundaries with their ex (limited number of shared friends, limited contact, etc.).
   Bonus sign: Your gut tells you no lingering feelings are haunting your relationship.

It's obvious that you want to meet someone who isn't hung up on anyone else, but the first step is making sure that you are available, too—and not hung up on anyone else.

How to make lingering feelings for an old flame vanish:

If you're still hung up on an old love, or if any part of you is still attached to them, that must be dealt with before you can enter a new relationship.

While it's easy to remember the good times and the dearest memories, it's very important to force yourself to recall the bad times, too. Think of the times they made you feel unloved. Think of the habits they had that you couldn't stand.

Remember the reasons why they just weren't the right person for you, why they didn't fit your dream scenario, and what it is that you're actually looking for.

Don't forget that the reason it didn't work out with this person is because you're meant to be with someone else.

You might have to distract yourself with some new hobbies or new activities, you might have to unfollow your ex from social media, and you may have to delete old photos and texts. Do whatever you need to do to move on so that you can be a clean slate for your next partner.

Never Date the Overly Mysterious Type

Another type of unavailable person you probably shouldn't date is the mysterious and guarded type. If you're dating someone who's difficult to get to know because they're mysterious and private rather than open and authentic, the relationship won't feel genuine at all. Gone are the days where you should feel attracted to someone ultra-mysterious. There's a difference between a subtle air of mystery in the beginning and dating a completely private, closed-off person who is difficult to get close to because they have serious baggage and major walls up.

No real connection or bond can be formed with the mysterious type which ultimately leads to a lack of chemistry and a failed relationship. You can definitely voice your concerns, encourage him or her to be more open, or explain that you're attracted to people who show their emotions—but a better idea is to not waste your time with the mysterious type in the first place. Here some reasons why you should never date the mysterious type:

You'll never really feel a close connection. The connection and the chemistry might both be present, but if you can't get them to open up you'll never be able to build a solid connection. If they won't let you get to know them, or if they don't really want you to get to know them, you'll never feel the close bond that amazing relationships are built on.

It will most likely be a surface-level relationship. When someone doesn't really let you in, you might be intrigued at first, but eventually, you realize it's preventing the two of you from having a legitimate, honest relationship. With the mysterious man or the mysterious woman, you're more likely to only have a surface-level relationship where you don't know each other that well, and you're doomed to forever remain in that gray area.

They'll probably be too passive for your liking. The quiet and mysterious types most likely won't feel confident voicing their opinions or being direct with you. Any chance they get, they'll take the passive route instead of the direct route. Women love dating direct men because they're transparent and speak their mind which makes dating them easy instead of complicated and stressful. Men love dating direct women because they're mature and confident.

You won't get to share their important milestones. If you're dating someone, you likely want to be kept in-the-know when it comes to the trials and tribulations of their life. You'll want them to call you when they get fantastic news, and you'll also want them to tell you when something bad happens. The mysterious, closed-off type will keep all that information (good and bad) to themselves instead of opening up and sharing their milestones with you. They might know that you care and that you'd want to hear about it, yet they remain private. The result? A pretty shitty relationship. The personality trait of being too private or too mysterious is your worst enemy when it comes to dating.

You won't feel encouraged to share *your* milestones. You might get super exciting news or sad news that you'll feel you can't share with your partner since they don't share. But why can't you? It's not that you can't share the news, it's more so that you won't want to because you get the vibe that they won't care. Considering this person isn't open enough to share his or her stories with you, you'll feel hesitant to share yours—and that's pretty discouraging.

Your conversations will lack engagement and depth. The mysterious, closed-off man or woman will often fail to be engaged in a conversation with you. Conversations will feel one-sided because while you might be open to having a deep conversation or sharing something very personal or significant, they won't want to do the same. Who wants to date someone who has poor conversational skills or lacks depth?

Passion will be scarce. The problem with the mysterious

type is that they don't feel comfortable showing emotion, so therefore, they won't feel comfortable showing passion or executing grand gestures. Translation? Don't expect any above-and-beyond effort or romantic surprises.

You'll never know what they're thinking and you won't feel comfortable asking. Dating the mysterious type is a constant mindf*ck and a continuous guessing game. You'll never be sure of where you stand with them, and you'll never really know what they're thinking or how they feel. Since they seem to be so stubbornly closed-off, you won't exactly feel comfortable asking, either. This is why you want to date someone open instead of wasting your time with the mysterious type.

Dating Unavailable People is Ruining your Shot at Real Love

Don't be someone's down-time, spare-time,
part-time or sometime.
If they can't be there for you all of the time,
then they're not even worth your time.
—Anonymous

By dating unavailable people over and over, you've kept yourself in dating purgatory. Purgatory, among other things, means the place in the afterlife between Heaven and Hell. When it comes to dating, Heaven would be that blissful feeling when you and your love interest are both extremely interested in each other. A dating Hell would be when the object of your desire couldn't be less interested in you.

Dating Purgatory is what I like to call it when a prospect is not super interested but not exactly disinterested, either. They're not fully available to you but not totally unavailable either.

Perhaps there is a visible interest but not enough to allow you to be sure of where you stand. It's something many men and women of our generation experience and for some reason, tolerate.

What we don't realize when we're starved for romance, though, is that if the way he or she feels about you isn't blatantly obvious, that's *not* good enough.

Dating Purgatory isn't where you want to be if you're in search of something real. Yet it's where a lot of us end up when we date unavailable people.

No substantial and worthwhile relationship can be built from an in-between, mediocre 'situationship.' That's why we can't waste our time with the lack-luster 'maybe relationships' anymore.

So when exactly are you in Dating Purgatory? It's whenever you have one foot out the door instead of jumping into a relationship with both feet. It's whenever you keep dating someone who wants nothing serious even though you do. It's when you date someone unavailable even though you're available.

It's when you're not all in, or they're not all in, or you're both not all in.

It's all those times we dated people never knowing where we stood, being unsure of how they felt, and not knowing whether or not they were seeing anyone else. It's whenever you find yourself in a relationship that has no label or anytime you find yourself in an unsatisfying almost-relationship.

Deep down, though, we all want the real thing; we all want to find love.

What does the real deal look like? Well, it involves self-sacrifice. It's giving up other options. It's when you jump in with both feet and give what you've got a real shot.

It's when you know exactly where you stand with each other—and there are no questions. You're not uncertain. You know what you've found is unbeatable.

We need to start focusing on the benefits of being in a relationship rather than mulling over the drawbacks or worrying about the sacrifices.

It requires bravery to decide you want to be committed to someone and to go into it without having anyone on the backburner.

It's terrifying for some people to cut ties with those they have on the backburner, but without doing it, you don't deserve the reward of a meaningful relationship.

You've got to train yourself to become more *resistant* to mediocrity. No more mediocre dates, mediocre relationships, or mediocre feelings.

You can't have anymore more pseudo-relationships with unavailable people if what you want is the real deal.

8

When It Comes To Love, Your Instincts Guide You More Than You Realize

The best and most beautiful things in this world cannot be seen or even heard but must be felt with the heart.
—Helen Keller

Intuition is an extremely powerful human phenomenon. When it comes to dating, relationships, and love, your instincts guide you more than you know.

You will subconsciously do everything in your power to stay single if your intuition is telling you that you're not ready to be in a relationship. If deep down you know that there's more you need to see, do, or experience before you're ready to be in a meaningful partnership, you'll sabotage your relationships to keep them at surface-level. You'll stand in your own way, you'll block people from getting in, you'll come up with excuses to avoid dating, and you'll stay single.

And, if you are ready for a relationship, your instincts will still guide you.

Whenever something feels off in a new relationship, explore that feeling. Listen to that voice in your head that says *something isn't right*. Your gut could be telling you that this isn't the right person for you, and listening to that gut instinct can help you avoid wasting your precious time. Tread carefully because most of the time, your intuition is on to something.

Sometimes, though, your intuition leads you to love. Hypothetically speaking, let's say you lined up a couple of dates this week. You went out with Blair and Morgan. Your gut whispers to you that there's something different about Blair—something very special. Maybe he or she isn't your usual type, yet you're drawn to him or her for an unexplainable reason.

> *All the learning in the world cannot replace instinct.*
> *—Robert Ley*

On paper, Morgan is your exact type. Morgan's personality, values, and physical appearance are all exactly what you're looking for—and yet you may feel nothing when you're with Morgan. You wish you could tell your heart who to fall in love with—but you can't. You can't tell your heart who to choose.

Love can't be explained. It's not a choice or a decision—it's a feeling. It's a pull. It can't be forced and sometimes it happens with someone you'd never expect it to happen with. That's what makes it so magical. If it feels right, go for it and don't play games or miss your window. Remember that your gut instinct is a gift and that it won't lead you astray. If you feel something special with someone and you don't pursue it, you'll be left with feelings of regret—and you'll feel like a coward.

Following a suppressed instinctual feeling requires courage, and it's this courage that gets you what you want in life.

Trust in what the future holds.

Even though you've been chronically single for what seems like forever, does your intuition whisper to you that the love of your life is out there and that you will find love? If so, you're on the right path. It's crucial to trust in what the future holds and to remain optimistic.

Whether you've been perpetually single (almost no relationships to date) or you've had a history of failed relationships (lots of breakups), both can be seen as a positive thing.

Perhaps your chronic singlehood is a good thing. It could mean that you're meant to have one fantastic relationship in your lifetime rather than a series of mediocre ones. You're meant to find true love instead of a lot of "I think it's love?"

And all that time to yourself while single has let you devote your resources to yourself, allowing for self-improvement and self-actualization that's beyond what others have ever reached. In a way, you overcompensate for being single. You perfect every other area of your life *because* you're single, and that's definitely not a bad thing.

Similarly, if a history of failed relationships has left you hopeful and optimistic, that means you have the right attitude towards dating, relationships, and love. Some people develop a negative attitude towards dating after a history of bad luck.

These people will bring that negativity with them into any new relationship, thus severely lowering the chances of that relationship working out.

Dating someone who has good instincts results in an amazing partnership.

It is rare to meet the type of person who is so intuitive that they have the ability to understand you without any offered explanations from you.

They have an uncanny intelligence when it comes to figuring you out. When you're uncomfortable or anxious, they know and can also tell when you're genuinely happy. They give a whole new meaning to "reading between the lines."

They might take notice of what types of situations seem to relax you and will remember what puts you in a good mood.

That way, when his or her intuition communicates that something seems off, it's a signal to attempt to help. If someone gets you like that, they are surely a keeper.

9

From Single To Taken Part 1: Newly Dating

*You may have a fresh start any moment you choose,
for this thing that we call 'failure' is not the falling down,
but the staying down.*
—*Mary Pickford*

When you do finally meet the right person, a whole new you has to manifest. You'll have to adapt, change, and re-identify with yourself. Transitioning from being very single to actually being in a committed relationship can be overwhelming, weird, exciting, and difficult at times. A lot is going to change now, for the better, but still! Change is always stressful. It might even feel awkward at first if you've 'forgotten' how to date or if you have trouble identifying with the version of you who is no longer single.

First, we'll discuss how to feel comfortable about dating someone new in general. Then, we'll move on to discuss what the transition is like from being single to being in a relationship.

Conquering Feelings of Awkwardness or Discomfort

What to do when you feel awkward or uncomfortable around someone you're newly dating:

It's completely normal to feel awkward or weird around someone you're newly dating. It's especially those first few dates that can make you feel uneasy, but there are ways to make sure your first few dates aren't awkward.

There's a lot more that goes into a successful date than just looking good and smelling good. We always hope we won't act odd, standoffish, or accidentally say something awkward or weird. You want the date to go smoothly, and you don't want to do anything that might turn off your date. It's never a good feeling to leave a date with someone you're interested in feeling as though it didn't go well and feeling certain you won't be seeing him or her again.

Sometimes, the first few dates are agonizing and uncomfortable, but you then start to learn what types of dates work for you and you notice which dates allow you to feel more at ease and therefore, less awkward.

If you want to make sure it's not awkward, plan ahead. Having a plan is one of the best ways to make sure your date will go smoothly. A lot of introverted people and socially awkward people rely on this dating strategy. Your date night plan should include things like reservations, a planned outfit, a set time, a meeting place, and a second location pre-planned in case the date is going well and you want to stay out.

Research things like comedy shows, karaoke bars, and don't shy away from reading reviews and asking around so that you know what you're getting into. It's a lot better than being surprised when a venue isn't at all what you expected. If you can, go on a reconnaissance mission so that you know what to expect, and if it doesn't go well, add it to your list of date locations to avoid.

An awkward person doesn't need the attention on them at all times on a date. Go to places like open-mic nights, karaoke bars, comedy clubs, and improv shows so that you can enjoy your date's company without feeling the pressure to make conversation all night long. Those distractions will be your best friend.

This means that you don't go anywhere too quiet, either. In general, the noisy buzz of people and music will help you get through an unnerving date, and that noise in the background will also help you not notice any awkward silences. An awkward silence feels ten times more awkward in a silent, empty restaurant. I'll tell you that much.

You don't want to go anywhere that's so loud that you can't hear each other talk, but you do want to pick a place that has a healthy level of background noise. Again, this is where research comes in handy. You'll get to know the restaurants and lounges that are always decently busy, not too loud, and not too quiet.

Going somewhere fancy is basically you asking for an awkward date. If you go someplace fancy, you'll feel even more uncomfortable and consumed with obsessive thoughts. At a fancy place, you'll be thinking, *Is what I'm wearing nice enough for this place?* And *Is it just me, or is it so quiet in here that it's getting awkward?* And *Am I using the right fork?* And *Am I going to have to pay for half of this expensive-ass bill?* Not to mention the fear that you didn't pronounce the menu item you ordered properly...

For some reason, you really feel the pressure and feel the expectations at a fancy place. You feel as though you must be on your best behaviour, and you end up not really being yourself. It's better to keep it casual for the first few dates until you're comfortable enough with each other to survive the white tablecloths and three forks.

It can be super awkward to go on an extremely romantic, extravagant, and intimate date in the beginning.

Lastly, avoid anywhere with lines on a date so that there are no awkward periods of time. Although going to the zoo or going to a theme park may seem like a good date idea, it's not. At least not until you're comfortable with that person. You're going to be waiting in long lines, and that can be awkward. Sometimes you're stuck in the sun and you're hot, sweaty, and not in the mood to make small talk while you wait in line. Plus, nobody *likes* waiting in lines, so maybe it's not as fun of a date idea as you think.

Now that you've figured out how to *start* dating without feeling weird about it, let's discuss how to build momentum, and then how to ultimately transition from being single to being off the market.

Why Momentum is So Important in Dating

Just as moving too fast can cause a relationship to fail, moving too slowly can definitely kill a new relationship's potential.

Your new relationship doesn't stand a chance unless you keep the momentum going. After a fantastic first date, you have something to work with. There's a powerful and positive energy that can be maintained after that incredible first date, but it's up to you to keep the momentum going. This is what I decided to call the Momentum Theory of Dating.

My Momentum Theory suggests that the first several dates should be in close succession to each other in order to better your chances of the relationship blossoming.

Not only will this mentality better your chances with a prospect, but it is also the best way to truly get to know someone and the best way to turn that spark into a flame.

This means that you shouldn't wait too long to plan the next date, you need to take initiative, and you should aim to maintain consistent contact with a prospect in between dates.

A slow progression or intermittent lulls of no contact in between dates can potentially kill your chances with someone. If you want it to eventually turn into something, you must keep the momentum going from the *beginning*. This certainly doesn't mean that you should rush anything—you simply want to take things at a steady pace.

While it is acceptable to go slow, moving *too* slowly can have adverse effects.

One of the most important traits to bring into a relationship is the trait of follow-through. People who follow through on what they say and follow through on plans are great partners.

The deceptive mindset that you have options can cause some of us to develop nonchalant attitudes when it comes to dating. Without coming across as overly eager, you must act with the mentality that progressing the relationship forward is vital to the success of that relationship.

If, for example, you're able to focus on driving your career forward, you simply need to manifest that same drive when it comes to your romantic endeavors. Rather than assuming no effort is needed to keep someone interested. instead, we should assume the opposite: not being on the ball can result in you getting kicked off the court.

The first several dates should be spaced close together in an effort to keep the momentum going. The second date should not take place more than two weeks after the first date. If the first date went exceptionally well, the best thing you can do is lock in a second date soon after. The following few dates should all be spaced as close together as possible.

Those who don't keep the momentum going after a fantastic first few dates are what I would call 'passive daters' or 'lazy daters.' You don't want to be one of them, trust me. The lazy courtship sucks, and nobody is impressed by it. Most of the great catches out there are completely turned off by passive, lazy daters. They want to meet someone who puts in the effort and keeps the momentum going.

If you enter into a new relationship and you fail to keep the momentum going, the initial butterflies you felt can lose their effect. The chemistry you feel on a first date needs to be maintained with a second date, third date, fourth date, and fifth date in close succession. Otherwise, you risk the momentum being lost and perhaps never regained. If you slow the momentum down, you'll be making your pursuit of this person much more difficult than it otherwise could be.

Lock down your next date well in advance if you want to show someone that you're mature and reliable. We all have busy schedules, and sometimes failing to anticipate how busy someone's calendar might be could be the cause of the momentum slowing down.

The best thing to do is to take initiative and say, "Are you free next Saturday night?" Giving someone a week's notice means they can reserve that entire evening for you and look forward to it all week. This is much more effective than passively waiting until the weekend rolls around and finding out he or she already has plans. Women definitely appreciate it when a man takes initiative like this; however, women should not hesitate in taking that initiative themselves from time to time.

Keep the momentum going through communication, too. Sending a text message every few days to check in and say hi is a great way to keep the momentum going, thus keeping the prospect interested in between dates.

Similar to how waiting longer too long to lock in your next date is detrimental, waiting too long in between contacting them can damage the relationship, too.

Moving too fast is not the goal. An insta-relationship almost never lasts. In order to avoid letting the relationship progress too quickly, you'll have to have self-discipline. The reason I say this is because your partner might try to hold your hand and drag you into a whirlwind romance, and you might have to be the one to slow things down. This requires self-discipline because it can be extremely tempting to take that jump instead of proceeding with caution. You never want to be too cautious, but you do need to keep in mind that for a relationship with potential to develop and reach that potential, you must take your time.

The goal is simply not to move too slowly while still making sure you don't move too fast. There is a happy medium which will be different for everyone. For example, the standard rule is that going longer than 5-7 days without texting someone you are interested in will send the wrong message and raise a red flag for them.

Remember: If you snooze, you just might lose. Nothing

good ever comes easily, so put some effort into your dating life. This way, you'll start a new relationship off on the right path.

"What Are We?"

So you're dating someone, right? You see them pretty often, you have fun, and you like each other. If you find yourself wondering, "What are we?" or "Where do I stand with this person?" it's time to have *the talk*.

People avoid that talk all the time. Whether it's because they're afraid of being rejected, afraid of awkwardness, or they're simply uncomfortable being vulnerable—people in new relationships avoid the talk all the time. I'm here to tell you to stop avoiding it.

In the past, perhaps you stayed in a non-relationship or an almost-relationship, and you never questioned what it was out of fear that the moment you asked any questions about what you are or where you stand, you'd scare that fragile pseudo-relationship away.

You were aware that the relationship wasn't stable, and you were afraid if you so much as blew on it, it'd be gone.

That's why you tiptoed around the issue of "What are we?" and danced around the question of "What do you want this to be?"

You shouldn't settle unless someone makes it clear that they want you, adore you, and would love to be exclusive with you. If someone's not all in and wants to keep one foot out the door, they obviously don't adore you.

You're too mature now to sidestep these pivotal conversations. You're too brave now to be fearful. As soon as you discuss the idea of being exclusive, you'll feel so much better. It has to be done, so stop avoiding the conversation.

10

From Single To Taken Part 2: Becoming A 'We'

When you realize you want to
spend the rest of your life with somebody,
you want the rest of your life
to start as soon as possible.
—Nora Ephron

If you're becoming a 'we' you'll be gaining certain benefits that come with the partnership and taking on certain disadvantages, as well. You won't lose sight of your individual identity and goals, so don't worry about that. If you're confident, strong, and in a great relationship with yourself, you won't lose yourself once you're in a relationship.

The Transition from Single to Taken

You'll have to get used to the idea of giving up your other

options. Remember that the perks of options don't outweigh the *huge* perk of being in a loving relationship. Oftentimes, the other options you think you're missing out on are actually a delusion, which is why you shouldn't let FOMO (the fear of missing out) get the best of you.

Now your partner might be bringing a lot of assets into the relationship. That being said, they might be bringing some minor issues into your life, too. These issues introduced to your life could include them having a cat when you're allergic to cats, them having a lingering ex or judgmental parents, or them having financial issues which means you can't do all the things you'd like to do together (unless you pay).

It's better for both of you if there are no uncomfortable and awkward surprises which means you need to ask direct questions if there's anything you're wondering about. You should also be clear with each other with regards to your expectations.

If it's important to you that your partner is financially stable, be careful when you meet someone who seems to have it all. You could meet someone who is asset-rich and cash poor, as they drive a nice car, own expensive clothes, and live as though they make over six figures. It could be a façade, and it's your prerogative to find out what's what. It's okay to want to date someone with their finances in order. It shows maturity, and it allows the two of you to have a lot more freedom in your relationship.

When you find yourself in a new relationship, you'll also need to set boundaries before that person decides to test your boundaries. Some people are totally fine with their partner being friends with their ex, for example. Don't assume they'll understand your expectations if you don't make them clear. Other boundaries to be discussed include things like using their toothbrush or not, how sexually adventurous you are, and how much 'me' time (space) you require. Everyone is different, so these things need to be communicated.

In fact, the number one thing that will help you transition from single to taken is your ability to clearly communicate.

When you're in a new relationship, is it important to get opinions from your friends and family?

Getting the opinion of others is actually a great idea when you've started dating someone new. Don't rush this—you don't want to move the relationship too fast by introducing them to the important people in your life too quickly. Before you get serious with someone, though, introduce him or her to your friends and some family members.

Your friends and family know you well, so their perspective on your new babe does count for something. They might fall in love with this new person you're dating, confirming what you already knew, or they may shed light on something you hadn't noticed or considered. Your new partner will be seeing a lot of your friends and family, so it's great if they get along, and an important step towards transitioning to a 'we.'

Allocating your time.

Going from single to taken is comparable to taking on a part-time job when you already have a full-time job or starting a new business venture when you already have a pretty full plate.

If you're saying sayonara to your single days, then you're also saying goodbye to a certain amount of free time—the time you spent doing your own thing. You probably won't be getting through season three of *Suits* quite as quickly as you otherwise would, nor will you have as many free nights to catch up on laundry or housework. You've always known the value of your time and spend it on what's important to you, and now a lot of it will go to your significant other because you value your relationship.

If you care enough about someone to give up singlehood, you probably care enough to reassign some of that time to them, as difficult as it may be. You need to be prepared to reassign some of your time, even if your single friends are disappointed about not holding ownership of your Saturday nights anymore.

The 11 Habits that Can Make or Break a Budding Relationship

When you meet someone amazing and you first start dating that person, suddenly you're in a budding relationship with great potential.

One of the most intimidating spots to be in is in a new relationship that has the possibility of becoming something wonderful. It's in that exciting, beginning phase when you haven't done anything wrong…but you can't help thinking of the word *yet*. You haven't done anything to scare them away *yet*. You haven't lost their interest *yet*. You haven't screwed up *yet*.

If you took the time to think about the habits that can make or break a new relationship and you became more conscious of those habits, would your budding relationship have a better chance of success? Probably. When someone incredible enters into your life, keep these 11 habits that can make or break a relationship in mind:

1. Make it clear that you have your own life. Never make the mistake of being overly attentive, too available, or extraflexible for the benefit of a new prospect. Anyone too easy to get is automatically less attractive, and you don't want it to seem as though you're scheduling your life around them. Instead, set aside time for your date while still making it clear that you have your own life. Let it be known that you have friends, hobbies, passions, a dedicated career, and a great life that you simply want this new person to be a part of. When you're starting a relationship, revolving your life around them or accommodating them too much is the last thing you want to do.

2. Don't give them everything too soon. You don't have to do cute things for them in the beginning or go out of your way for them just yet. This encourages them to make an effort to get to know you on a deeper level and allows them to pursue you. You also shouldn't get physical too soon. You want your new flame to place a high value on your affection which won't happen if they never had to earn it. Remember, it's important to give them a chance to *pursue* you.

3. Go out on real dates. Don't get into the habit of suggesting a boring date-night-in every time you make plans. While it's okay to stay home and watch Netflix sometimes, the happiest and healthiest couples go out on unique, exciting, and memorable dates. Going for drinks, going for coffee, and watching a movie at home are mediocre dates that don't require much thought. Instead, try getting creative and coming up with something that might actually be memorable. The couples who share fun and special experiences are the couples who will form the strongest bond and associate each other with a good time. Never allow one person in the relationship to come up with all the date ideas. Both of you should surprise each other and take the lead when it comes to planning fun outings.

4. Make an effort to keep your conversations interesting. Again, this all goes back to effort. You need to put effort into new relationships but in the most subtle of ways. For example, the conversation that takes place on your dates should always be stimulating and interesting. If something happened to you this week that would make a great story, save it for your next date. Don't talk about it in a text message, because you want to tell your best stories when you're face-to-face. You'll also want to let them talk about themselves, and actively listen.

Don't just ask your date about their job, their dog, or what they like to do for fun. This just proves that you're not capable of real, deep conversation.

If you really want to stand out and impress your date, ask some real questions. Asking questions is what makes a conversation interesting and intriguing. Ask about their goals, dreams, fears, passions, and proudest achievements. Showing a genuine interest in your date will go a long away, and people tend to light up when they're discussing what's most important in their life such as their goals and their passions. Ask leading questions about what they're proudest of and what excites them—and let them see that you're genuinely keen on getting to know them. Interesting conversation helps keep your admirer interested, too.

5. Communicate maturely from the beginning. In relationships, especially new ones, your communication habits can make or break its momentum. It also requires an ability to be direct and straightforward with your partner rather than sugarcoating, beating around the bush, or being too afraid to speak up. Healthy couples have no problem being direct with each other. They avoid being passive and will always tell each other when something major is bothering them. Real talk is back in style. This doesn't mean you nag about everything that bothers you, though.

6. Pick your battles. It's important that you don't nag your partner about every little thing that pisses you off. Even if something they said or did slightly upsets you, sometimes you just have to let it go without saying a word about it. Save your nagging for when something *really* bothers you, otherwise, you'll end up being the bothersome one 99% of the time. As far as speaking up goes, there are ways to verbalize your feelings without sounding whiney. For any relationship to have a shot at success, both parties must remember to pick their battles and not sweat the small stuff.

7. Be reliable and follow through on your word. If you want to be deemed dateable, you need to stop being late, stop canceling plans, and stop changing plans (unless it's a change in the form of an upgrade—in which case, that's fine.) Say what you mean and mean what you say. Everyone wants to date someone they can count on, and nobody wants to date someone who's flaky.

8. Discover common interests. If you both enjoy similar hobbies and you share common interests, you have a real shot at making your relationship last. Going to the gym together, hiking together, exploring your city together, and discovering new restaurants with each other are all great ways to solidify common ground. Shared interests can strengthen your bond as a couple, and experiencing cool and unique activities together will keep things fun and exciting.

9. Don't overshare too soon. The getting-to-know-each-other process can be ruined if you get too comfortable too soon. Avoid oversharing because when you overshare personal and intimate details about your life or about your past, you're crossing a boundary that perhaps wasn't ready to be crossed yet. Remind yourself that there will be plenty of time later in the relationship to share these things.

10. Needing constant reassurance to quiet your insecurities is not attractive. Everyone is attracted to confident, self-assured people who don't rely on others for happiness or security. By needing constant reassurance from your partner and by showcasing insecurities, you'll drive them away. It's not enjoyable to feel as though your partner needs more of you than you're willing to give.

11. Keep the momentum going. The key to fostering a connection is to keep the relationship moving at a steady pace. Keep the momentum going without falling behind or moving too fast. As we just discussed, momentum is incredibly important in new relationships.

Remember that You're Ready

In Chapter 1, we discussed the signs that you're ready to be in a relationship. One of those signs was when you come to realize that the way you act when you're single would actually closely match the way you would act if you were in a relationship.

This theory holds a different meaning for different people. For example, for some of you, it could mean that you've completely gotten promiscuity out of your system and you no longer have one night stands, nor do you go out on the prowl anymore. For others, this 'relationship-like' single behaviour could include you cooking delicious meals for one when there's always enough for two. Or maybe you've been participating in plenty of activities where most of the participants bring a plus-one and you're one of the few who doesn't.

Remember that you're pursuing this relationship because you're ready for it. You're ready to be part of a couple. You want this new adventure, and this new chapter, to start as soon as possible. You're more than willing to give up your other prospects and you've been looking for a plus-one to bring to those events. Reminding yourself that you're ready for this will help with the transition from being single to being in a relationship.

An Incredible Relationship is Worth All of the Effort and Sacrifices

Opening your heart and sharing it means that you're going to get so much love in your life. It's the way to true connection and real purpose and meaning in your life.
—Amy Poehler

Healthy relationships help you find fulfillment in life. You get to share your life with someone who witnesses all of your highs and lows and *gives a damn* about them. Every special occasion in a calendar year becomes *extra* special when you're in a relationship. And now you've got an activities partner, someone to confide in, someone to plan vacations with, someone to set goals with, someone to have fantastic sex with, someone to cuddle with, someone to go on unforgettable dates with, someone who emotionally supports you...I could go on. Let's just say that there could be a whole book about the benefits of a being in a relationship, one that would convince every perpetually single man and woman to want one.

So obviously, the sacrifices you make to be in a relationship are worth it. These sacrifices include giving up other options, giving up some of your free time, and risking getting hurt.

Casual dating was appealing at one time in your life or another. It was appealing because it was so low-risk and required such little effort. The casual non-relationship also guarantees that there won't be that hurtful breakup if things don't work out.

But, as the old saying goes, *no pain, no gain*—and what you can gain is an amazing relationship with true intimacy and the sense of happiness and fulfillment that comes with it. (Plus, the best sex of your life will be with someone you're truly intimate with who knows what and where your buttons are.) These tremendous gains are worth the risks and sacrifices, there's no doubt about it.

Deep down, we all want to meet someone who treats us like a priority instead of an option. We all want to be with someone who makes us feel valued and important and special. Deep down, we all want to connect, because connecting with someone is what makes us feel alive.

Finding a meaningful partnership was a lot easier for our parents and grandparents. That's because online dating was less prevalent, and people had fewer options getting in the way of commitment, fewer filters getting in the way of reality, and fewer distractions causing chronic absenteeism.

All you have to do is talk to your parents and your grandparents if you want to hear stories of a time when more people gave it their all and actually openly communicated their feelings with each other. The most successful relationships of our generation stem from an old-fashioned courtship and an old-fashioned romance.

I think it's safe to say that as human beings, our inherent desire for love and intimacy are the same desires of the more romantic, older generations. It's just that our generation's ability to acknowledge and act upon those desires has gone downhill. Every single one of you, however, can choose to act now and grab hold of the love that you deserve. It'll be worth it, I promise, and now that you've read this book—you're *so* ready.

About the Author

Erica Gordon has been working in the dating industry for over six years, and her influential voice has become prominent and respected throughout North America, Australia, and the U.K. From working at the headquarters of some of the world's largest dating sites to running *The Babe Report* (thebabereport.com)—her dating advice column for Millennials—and freelancing as a dedicated dating coach, her expertise is in all things dating and relationships. After Erica earned her Psychology degree from the University of British Columbia, she pursued writing by virtue of the endorsement of her prof. The very first article she wrote went viral, and she's never slowed down since. She was recently quoted as a dating expert in *Vanity Fair*, and today, she combines her love of writing and her passion for giving dating advice by writing advice pieces for several of the world's largest online magazines, including *Elite Daily*, *AskMen*, *Huffington Post* and *Thought Catalog*. As a Millennial on the cusp of being a Gen X'er, both generations can relate to Erica's writing—and her advice is so spot on, you'll wonder if she's inside your head. If you want to ask Erica an advice-related question, you can find *The Babe Report* on Twitter @thebabereport, Facebook (facebook.com/thebabereport), or Instagram @the_babe_report.

YOU MIGHT ALSO LIKE:

Everything You Need To Know If You Want Love That Lasts
by Sabrina Alexis

Love S.U.C.K.S. (Seems Unusually Confusing & Kinda Scary) by Isis
Nezbeth

The First New Universe by Heidi Priebe

THOUGHT CATALOG

IT'S A WEBSITE.

www.thoughtcatalog.com

SOCIAL

facebook.com/thoughtcatalog
twitter.com/thoughtcatalog
tumblr.com/thoughtcatalog
instagram.com/thoughtcatalog

CORPORATE

www.thought.is